# ECONOMIC EFFICIENCY IN PULSES CULTIVATION

# ECONOMIC EFFICIENCY IN PULSES CULTIVATION

*By*

**Dr. D. Amutha**

*Assistant Professor*
*Dept. of Economics*
*St. Mary's College*
*Tuticorin, Tamil Nadu*
*(India)*

**DISCOVERY PUBLISHING HOUSE PVT. LTD.**

**NEW DELHI-110 002**

*Published by:*
**Tilak Wasan**
**DISCOVERY PUBLISHING HOUSE PVT. LTD.**
4383/4B, Ansari Road, Darya Ganj
New Delhi-110 002 (India)
*Phone* : +91-11-23279245, 43596064-65
*Fax* : +91-11-23253475
*E-mail* : parul.wasan@gmail.com
discoverypublishinghouse@gmail.com
*web* : www.discoverypublishinggroup.com

***First Edition:* 2013**

**ISBN: 978-93-5056-312-0**

**Economic Efficiency in Pulses Cultivation**



*Printed at:*
Dynamic Printers
Delhi

*DEDICATED TO*

**Rev. Dr. Sister. AVELIN MARY. FIBR., F.L.S.**

*Scientist & Director*

*Sacred Heart Marine Research Centre*

*Thoothukudi*

# Foreword

I read with great pleasure the book entitled *"Economic Efficiency in Pulses Cultivation"* by Ms. D.Amutha. The author has made an elaborate survey of the places in Tamil Nadu where pulses are cultivated. It is informative that the pulses crops are extensively grown in Nagapattinam, Thiruvarur, Cuddalore, Thoothukudi, Tirunelvi and Villupuram districts. The book presents state-wise area, output and yield of pulses in India. The productivity of pulses is highest in Nagaland.

The author in clear form presents the types of grams cultivated in different parts of Tamil Nadu with their annual production in tonnes. When the author wishes to focus on district wise cultivation of pulses, she concentrates on Thoothukudi district. While reading the thesis I understand that Thoothukudi district in Tamil Nadu is one of the most important districts where there has been a significant progress for cultivation of pulses and that in almost all the seven taluks in this district pulse cultivation is in practice. Producing black and green grams and to identify and analyse the determinants of yield and factors causing yield gap with regard to farmers cultivating two crops of pulses and of small and large farmers group and to estimate and analyse the input demand elasticity and supply responsiveness of two groups of farmers cultivating black and green grams and to investigate the labour absorption capacity and supply responsiveness of each group with regard to their own prices and prices of variable inputs and units of fixed inputs and also to study the nature and returns to scale for both black and green grams cultivating farmers.

Although the author had wished to collect data from large number of respondents, she could collect data from only 300 respondents due to lack of money, energy and time. The information required for the research was collected by survey method through personal interview with sample farmers, who were not maintaining detailed accounts on farming and the information on costs and return was elicited from their memory and experience. These farmers were using ancient methods for cultivation. But the author could derive from them the correct information by a method of extraction.

It is very important to read from the book that the author has made several suggestions to improve the production of pulses and the incentives to be given to farmers to achieve this. In short the work is a great contribution to the field of croup production. I congratulate the author to bring out a good book.

**Prof. Dr. P. Ananthakrishnan**

*Formerly Prof. & Head*

*Department of Chemistry*

*Anna University*

*Chennai - 600 025*

*Advisor*

*Sri Krishna Group of Engineering Institutions*

*Chennai - 601 301*

# Preface

People are becoming nutrition conscious. Print and electronic media pour out nutrition messages to the public. Pulses being rich source of protein form a very important part of vegetarian diet required for human health. If consumed with rice, they supply a good quantity of protein and some essential amino acids. Black Gram and Green gram is an important pulse crop of India with a wide soil and climatic adaptability. The book highlights the cost and returns, determinants of yield and supply responsiveness of selected pulses production. This book examines the input demand elasticities, the labour absorption capacity and returns to scale in Black Gram and Green Gram of pulses cultivation. The best result would be if I conclude that small farmers are economically more efficient than large farmers irrespective of varieties of pulses cultivation. Finally, this book focuses on the efficient allocation of inputs, direct supervision and farm management are crucial determinants of economic efficiency. It will be a practical guide for both present and future policy-makers in deciding on potential price-stabilizing interventions, and will also serve as a useful resource for researchers and students in agricultural economics. I hope that the book will serve as a useful reference document on the agricultural economics subject. I hope that every reader will enjoy reading this book. Any suggestion to further improve its contents is most welcome.

**Author**

# Acknowledgement

I would like to express my heartiest thanks to my Husband Mr. S.Joseph Benedict for his advice, encouragement and well wishes at all stages of the work.

I am indebted to my Mother Mrs. Theresammal Dasan and my Brother Mr. T.D. Mano Bharathi, Dinamani, Chennai, who has been a source of inspiration to me in my academic career. Their help and guidance both in my personal and academic life can neither be listed nor be quantified.

My special thanks are due to my sister Mrs. Helen and her sons Master Arockia Emerson and Master Arul Edmond, for their constant encouragement and well wishes.

I express my heartfelt thanks to my Mother-in-law Mrs. Siluvaikani Soosai Michael, for her advice, encouragement and well wishes at all stages of the work.

I would like to record my sincere thanks to the Principal, the Secretary and the Staff, St. Mary's College (Autonomous), Thoothukudi, for their help and encouragement to complete my work.

Above all, I thank and praise the Lord Almighty for His tender mercies and grace which He showered upon me to complete this research study.

**Dr. D. Amutha**

# Contents

*Foreword*

*Preface*

*Acknowledgement*

1. **Introduction** 1

Introduction; Pulses Production in India; Recent Trends in Seed Production in Pulses; Pulses Production in Tamil Nadu; Pulses Cultivation in Thoothukudi District; Statement of the Problem; Objectives of the Study; Limitations of the Study; Chapter Scheme

2. **Review of Literature and Concepts** 24

Review of Literature; Concepts

3. **Methodology and Profile of the Study Area** 58

Methodology; Profile of the Study Area

4. **Analysis of Cost and Return Structure** 73

Characteristics of Sample Farmers; Labour Utilisation and Input Output Structure; Cost and Returns Structure

5. **Determinants of Yield, Yield Gap and Constraints** 96

The Analytical Framework; Estimated Results of Regression Model for Black Gram; Test for Structural Differences; Tests of the Stability of Intercept and Scope; Estimated Results of Regression Model for

Green Gram; Test for Structural Differences; Tests of the Stability of Intercept and Slope; Yield Gap and Yield Constraints; Yield Constraints

**6. Impact of Black Gram on Input Demand Elasticities, Supply Responsiveness, Labour Absorption and Factor Shares** **115**

The Analytical Framework; Analysis of Black Gram (BG); Supply and Demand Elasticities; Indirect Estimates of Production Elasticities; Analysis of Green Gram (GG); Own and Cross Price Elasticities of Demand for Labour; Own and Cross Price Elasticities of Demand for Variable Inputs; Own and Cross Price Elasticities of Output Supply Green Gram (GG); Indirect Estimates of Production Elasticities; Impact of Black Gram (BG) on Factor Shares; Comparative Analysis of BG and GG Farmers' Groups

**7. Summary of Findings, Conclusion and Suggestions** **140**

Introduction; Summary of Findings; Conclusion; Suggestions

*Bibliography* *151*

*Index* *159*

# CHAPTER 1

# Introduction

## INTRODUCTION

Pulses are an important component of Indian diet in the predominantly vegetarian society. Besides being a rich source of protein, they are also important for sustainable agriculture. Pulses are having a rich source of protein required for human health. The average requirement of protein per head per day for each kg of body weight of the human being is 1 gm.

India is one of the largest producers, importers and consumers of pulses in the world accounting for 25 per cent of the global production, 15 per cent trade, and 27 per cent consumption, as sizeable population in the country still depends on vegetarian diets to meet its protein requirement.

Pulses like rice are the universal crops in the world, rated as one among the important crops because of their biological nitrogen fixing mechanism, inherited in situ and high protein contribution.

Among the merits of these crops, rich diversity in germplasm — adaptability to a variety of edapho-climatic conditions and its flexibility to accommodate itself in any cropping system need special mentioning.

However pulses' productivity is far below compared to that of food cereal crops. In India, even though it is cultivated over 1/5th of total cultivated area, its production is only 1/2nd of total food production. The reasons for this lower production is lower yield potential, cultivation of marginal lands, below average management efforts, non-availability of quality seeds, prevalence of higher temperature, susceptible to pod borers and wilt diseases are important.

## PULSES PRODUCTION IN INDIA

India is the largest producer and consumer of pulses in the world accounting for 33 per cent of the world area and 22 per cent of world production of pulses[1]. The domestic demand and consumption, however is much more than production mainly because pulses are a major source of protein for a large section of the vegetarian population in the country. The cultivation of pulses also provides of large quantity of green fodder, which serves as the nutritious food for the livestock. Besides their high nutritional value, pulse crops have unique characteristics of containing and restoring soil fertility through biological nitrogen fixation. In Tamilnadu, area wise, black gram occupies predominant place next to the green gram and red gram. The following practices may be adopted in different agro climatic zones for enhancing the pulses seed production by better utilization of the available resources.

Pulses in India have long been considered as the poor man's only source of protein. Pulses are grown in 22-33 million hectares of the area with an annual production of 13-15 million tons (mt). The growth rate of area under pulse crops is just 0.04 per cent during the period 1967-68 to 2009; as a result pulses' share in the total food grain production has reduced from 17 per cent in 1961 to 7 per cent in 2009. The major pulse crops grown in India are chickpea, pigeon pea, lentil, moongbean, black gram, green gram, and cowpea, urban and field pea. About 90 per cent of the global pigeon pea, 65 per cent of chickpea and 37 per cent of lentil area falls in India, corresponding to 93 per cent, 68 per cent and 32 per cent of the global production, respectively. Due to stagnant production, the net availability of pulses has come down from 60 gm/day/person in 1951 to 31gm/day/person in 2009.

The major pulse producing states are Madhya Pradesh (23 per cent), Uttar Pradesh (18 per cent), Maharashtra (14 per cent), Rajasthan (11 per cent) Andhra Pradesh (9 per cent), and Karnataka (6 per cent) where pulses are mostly grown as rainfed crops.

Domestic production of pulses after its peak of 14.94 million tonnes in 2003- 04 had declined to 13.38 million tonnes in 2004-05 and to 13.11 million tonnes in 2005-06 due to adverse climatic conditions prevalent in the major production zones. In the current year the production is estimated to increase marginally 14.1 million tonnes. This still falls short of domestic requirement of 17 million tonnes. But it will be increasing consistently with growing population, rising income value addition and market opportunities.

In India, the irrigated area under pulses was only 12 per cent, while under wheat and paddy; it was more than 60 per cent of the total area. Another critical input, credit was Rs 85 /ha for pulses, whereas it was Rs 458/ha for paddy and Rs 90/ha for wheat in 2001. To meet the demand for pulses, India has been importing a large quantity of pulses in recent years. The import of pulse crops increased from 0.38 Mt in 1993 to 2.8 Mt in 2008 (about 16 per cent of the domestic consumption). The widening gap in demand and supply has led to soaring prices of pulses during the past two years. Inclusion of pulses in future trading and limited availability in the international market have further fuelled price rise.

In the wake of green revolution the area under pulses experienced a drastic reduction in the Indo-Gangetic plains from 10.8 million ha in 1971-73 to 6.90 million ha in 2003-05.

By the development of appropriate production technologies, area under pulses in central and south India has however witnessed significant upward trend from 11 million hectares to 15.3 million hectares and thus recovering the area lost in the north India.

Last year, the ICAR Indian council for Agricultural Research produced 6.984 q breeder seed of 230 improved varieties of different pulse crops, 21 per cent more than the indent. However the efforts have been still inadequate in meeting the seed requirement mainly due to poor conversion of breeder seeds into foundation and certified seeds, i.e. 5.70 per cent against the target of 15 per cent. Thus there is a need to launch farmers' participatory seed production system across the country involving different stakeholders. Area of Black gram cultivation in Tamilnadu is 3.67 LHA and subsequently Green gram is 1.63 LHA, Red gram is 1.41 LHA Horse grams is 1.23 LHA, Bengal gram is 0.09 LHA and other pulses are cultivated in 1.50 LHA.

Pulses are not only the important food grain to supply protein which forms part of the vegetarian diet, but also are useful in many ways. It is a rich source of protein and possesses 2-3 times more than that of many other cereals. The protein composition makes up the deficiency of essential amino acids in cereals and millets. (Table 1.1).

**Table 1.1: Nutrient Content Pulses**

| Nutrient/Pulses | Red Gram | Black Gram | Green Gram | Bengal Gram | Soya Bean |
|---|---|---|---|---|---|
| Moisture (%) | 13.4 | 10.9 | 10.1 | 9.9 | 8.1 |
| Protein (%) | 22.3 | 24.0 | 24.5 | 20.8 | 43.2 |
| Fat (%) | 1.7 | 1.4 | 1.2 | 5.6 | 19.5 |
| Carbohydrates (%) | 57.6 | 59.6 | 59.9 | 59.8 | 20.9 |
| Minerals (%) | 3.5 | 3.2 | 3.5 | 2.7 | 4.6 |
| Calcium (mg) | 73.0 | 154.0 | 75.0 | 56.0 | 240.0 |
| Phosphorus (mg) | 304.0 | 385.0 | 45.0 | 331.0 | 690.0 |
| Iron (mg) | 5.8 | 9.1 | 8.5 | 1.1 | 11.5 |
| Total N (%) | 3.6 | 4.2 | 3.9 | 3.3 | 6.9 |
| Calorie value | 335.0 | 347.0 | 451.0 | 372.0 | 432.0 |
| Vitamin "A" (mg/100g) | 220.0 | 64.0 | 83.0 | 2160.0 | 710.0 |

Pulses enrich the soil fertility by fixing atmospheric nitrogen in the root nodules and improve the soil structure (Asthana and chaturvedi, 1999). The tap root system opens the soil into deeper strata and heavy leaf protein increases the soil organic matter and improves the soil structure. Pulses are an ideal crop for mixed and intercropping and also serve as nutritious vegetables and fodders. The seeds of lablab, peas, pigeon pea and chickpeas are used as green vegetables while mungbean, urd bean and cowpea are used as green fodders for cattle.

India, the subcontinent is growing pulses in about 22.39 million ha with a production of 14 – 24 million tonnes of pulses. This works out to an average productivity of 1623 kg/ha (1999). However India's rank in productivity is low, 24th in chickpea, 9th in pigeon pea, 23rd in lentil and 98th in total pulses. Andhra Pradesh, Gujarat, Karnataka, Madhya Pradesh, Maharashtra, Orissa, Rajasthan, Tamilnadu and Uttar Pradesh are the important states which grow the pulses in area ranged from 9.10 (Bihar) to 51.70 lakh ha (Madhya Pradesh). (Table 1.2).

**Table 1.2: State-wise Area, Output and Yield of Pulses**

| State | Area (L/ha) | Output (l/t) | Yield (kg/ha) |
|---|---|---|---|
| 1 | 2 | 3 | 4 |
| Andhra Pradesh | 16.10 | 8.38 | 477 |
| Arun. P | 0.07 | 0.07 | – |
| Assam | 0.98 | 0.51 | 520 |
| Bihar | 9.10 | 7.45 | 671 |
| Goa | 0.10 | 0.08 | – |
| Gujarat | 9.20 | 6.64 | 721 |
| Haryana | 4.20 | 3.45 | 823 |
| H.P | 0.72 | 0.11 | – |
| J & K | 0.35 | 0.17 | 470 |
| Karnataka | 17.50 | 7.22 | 382 |

*(Contd...)*

| 1 | 2 | 3 | 4 |
|---|---|---|---|
| Kerala | 0.21 | 0.15 | 800 |
| Madhya Pradesh | 51.70 | 35.44 | 719 |
| Maharashtra | 33.30 | 20.37 | 613 |
| Meghalaya | 0.03 | 0.03 | – |
| Mizoram | 0.04 | 0.07 | – |
| Nagaland | 0.08 | 0.14 | 1070 |
| Orissa | 8.50 | 2.26 | 350 |
| Punjab | 1.03 | 0.80 | 540 |
| Rajasthan | 38.00 | 18.45 | 494 |
| Sikkim | 0.07 | 0.06 | – |
| Tamil nadu | 9.50 | 2.33 | 430 |
| Tirpura | 0.07 | 0.06 | 924 |
| Uttar Pradesh | 28.80 | 26.25 | 672 |
| West Bengal | 2.30 | 1.72 | – |
| A & N Islands | 0.20 | 0.01 | – |
| D & N Haveli | 0.04 | 0.03 | – |
| Daman, Diu | 0.01 | 0.01 | – |
| Delhi | 0.02 | 0.02 | – |
| Pondicherry | 0.06 | 0.04 | – |
| All India | 223.90 | 142.44 | 623 |

*Source:* Economic Survey, 2010.

The average productivity of pulses ranged from 350 (Orissa) to 1070 kg ha (Nagaland). This productivity is very low when compared to cereals, millets and oilseeds. The annual production growth of pulses is estimated to be only 0.3 per cent when compared to 2.6 per cent in cereals. The current productivity level of pulse is very low which could not meet the per capita requirement of pulses i.e.; 80 gms day as recommended by the FAO/WHO. The current per capita availability of pulses is below 40 grams.

The requirement of protein in Indian diet has to be met through pulses especially for the vegetarians. The country will need 30.3 million tons of pulses by 2020 AD since the population will touch 1350 million by that time. But the pulses production remains stagnated for about 4 decades which should be increased through many possible approaches.

The following are the main reasons for the low productivity of pulses in India.

1. out of 22.39 million ha, about 78 per cent of the area is under rain fed conditions;
2. the soil where the pulse crops are grown are highly low in their nutrition level;
3. unfavourable weather conditions like erratic and uncertain rainfall, low and high temperature and moisture stress at various crop growth stages;
4. poor soil fertility and moisture retention capacity;
5. soil salinity and alkalinity;
6. the protein rich pulse crops are highly susceptible to various pests and diseases;
7. number of storage grain pests cause considerable losses;
8. lack of high yielding pest and disease tolerant pulse varieties;
9. farmers devote poor attention to the pulses cultivation;
10. mostly grown as mixed crop, intercrop, bund crop etc.;
11. lack of fine tuned package practices for pulses cultivation;
12. highly susceptible to drought and water logged conditions;
13. poor storability and lack of storage facility; and
14. fluctuation in the weather conditions affect the crop very much.

## Rice Fallow Pulses

Pulses are cultivated under irrigated as well as rainfed conditions. They are cultivated in another unique ecosystem knows as "rice fallow condition". In the residual soil moisture in this system, the pulses particularly black gram (Urd) and green gram (Mungbean) are broadcast, 7-10 days before the harvest of paddy crop and allowed to germinate and grow.

Since pulses are grown under paddy stubbles the pulse crops have to survive on the residual moisture in the soil, besides that, frost & mist available during the period will provide for the comfortable growth and yield within 65- 70 days of sowing. However, the yield recorded in this ecosystem is highly variable and depends on the management practices followed. The yield ranged from 300-500 kg/ha, this reduced production obtained from rice fallow pulses is due to:

- Very low extent of cultivation
- Sowing is not done at the appropriate time (January 15 – February 15)
- Use of poor quality seed with low germination (farmers seed)
- Poor seed and poor population
- Prevalence of drought during the reproductive stage
- Full of weeds
- Non practice of DAP spraying
- High pest and disease incidence

Besides, black gram, green gram and soya bean were introduced as rice fallow crop; but this is a highly sensitive crop to high temperature (34C) particularly at reproductive stage. The soya bean crop develops pods without seeds due to high temperature if prevailed during the reproductive stage. It has caused heavy loss to the farmers, which inhibited further promotion of soya bean area and cultivation in Cauvery delta zone of Tamilnadu.

Rice fallow area is a potential one, therefore careful and appropriate management of pulse crops will increase the yield. There is every possibility to expand the area of rice fallow with the pulses.

Like Rice, Cereals, Oilseeds, Millets etc., research outcome for the benefit of increasing yield in pulses is not much. Particularly biotechnological approach to get pulses resistant to biotic and abiotic stresses coupled with high yield is very minimal. However, if the following recommendations are followed the pulses' production can be increased.

## RECENT TRENDS IN SEED PRODUCTION IN PULSES

### Land Requirement

The land should be fertile and should not have grown the same crop in the previous season. If grown, it should be the same variety, which was certified for the said class of seeds. The land should be free from volunteer plants.

### Seeds and Sowing

The seeds should be obtained from an authenticated source with tag and bill. The off colour seeds should be removed from normal coloured, since they record lower germination. Only graded seeds should be used. In green gram and black gram the hard seed percentage may exceed to 10 per cent at a time.

At that time seeds should be scarified with commercial sulphuric acid for 2 minutes and should be washed thoroughly and used for sowing. If the field is infected with Macrophomina sp, the seeds are to be treated with Trichoderma @ 2 4g $kg^{-1}$.

Specific rhizobium strains (600 g $ha^{-1}$ as seed treatment) may be used for all pulses for increasing the yield, for better nodulation and maintenance of organic matter in the soil. Phosphobacteria @ 600 g $ha^{-1}$ as seed treatment is recommended for increasing the phosphorus use efficiency.

The seeds have to be treated with thiram or captan @ 2.0 g $kg^{-1}$ and insecticide carbary @ 200 mg $kg^{-1}$ before sowing for early protection against diseases and insects.

### Seed Hardening – cum – Invigouration Treatment of Pulses

The process of seed hardening followed by invigoration is given as pre-sowing seed treatment. This treatment enables (or) helps the pulses seed to germinate early with the available soil moisture. The hardened –cum-invigourated seeds will withstand besides drought much sowing better than the untreated seeds.

The invigoration process accelerates seedling growth and suppresses the weed growth. Better and early germination result in higher population per unit area and contribute to higher yield. Two seed management practices namely seed hardening and invigouration are combined in one process using cheap and easily available materials. The steps involved are:

**Seed Hardening – Pre-conditioning**

The seeds are pre-conditioned by placing them in between two moist gunny bags for a period of 1 hr., the gunny bags are first soaked in water, and then excess water is removed by squeezing and used for pre-conditioning. The seeds are spread to a depth of 1 to 2 cm on the gunny bag. After pre-conditioning the seeds are soaked in botanical solution as explained below:

**Soaking and Drying**

The pre-conditioned seeds are soaked in aqueous botanical leaf extracts of prosopis and pungam using 1 per cent solution each and taken in 1:1 ratio or mixed in 1:1 ratio. For example, to prepare 1 lit. of botanical extract, weigh 10 g each of prosopis and pungam fresh leaves, macerate it to a paste and make up the volume to 1 lit. of water. Soak the pre-conditioned seed in this prepared solution using 1:0.3 ratios. That is for 1 kg of seeds 300 ml of leaf extract is required.. Gently stir these seeds occasionally to enable uniform absorption. After 1 hr. drain the solution and dry the seeds in the shade.

**Invigouration**

Following seed hardening the seeds are treated with halogen formulation at 3 g $kg^{-1}$ of seed. Halogen formulation is prepared by taking 5 parts of pure bleaching powder with 4 parts of finely powdered chalk powder and 1 part of arappu leaf powder and mixed in a closed container. This treatment can be given to the seeds at the time of drying (When the surface moisture is removed) and then dried back to safe moisture level.

The treated seeds can be sown immediately or can be stored up to 1 week prior to sowing. Palanisamy and

Jayaseelan (1998)[2] found that pre-sowing seed treatments of red gram CV CO5 seeds with trichoderma @ 4 g kg$^{-1}$ followed by Rhizonbium culture inoculation at 24 hrs interval and subsequently pellating with ZnSo4 (100 mg kg$^{-1}$) using gypsum (300 g) as carrier and Maida 10 per cent (50 ml) as adhesive resulted in higher germination, seedling group, vigour index and field emergence (Table 1.3).

Vijaya and Ponnusamy (1998)[3] studied seed fortification and pelleting on crop growth and yield in black gram CV CO BG 282/1 and found that black gram seeds fortified with $ZnSo_4$ (0.2%) + $NaSo_4$ (0.2%) + Na2 $Mo_4$ (0.1%) and subsequently pelleting with DAP @ 120 g kg$^{-1}$ of seed registered higher yield and quality.

**Table 1.3: Effect of Seed Treatment in Redgram CV CO5**

| Treatment | Germination (%) | Root Length (cm) | Shoot Length (cm) | Vigour Index | Field Emergence (%) |
|---|---|---|---|---|---|
| $ZnSo_4$ (100 ppm) + Thira m (2g) + Rhizobium | 87.5 | 17.10 | 28.40 | 3978 | 84.00 |
| $ZnSo_4$ + trichoderma + Rhizobium | 88.5 | 17.70 | 28.60 | 4096 | 85.00 |
| Trichoderma + Rhizobiu m + $ZnSo_4$ Pellating | 98.0 | 18.20 | 31.40 | 4687 | 91.00 |
| Control | 84.0 | 17.00 | 28.70 | 3906 | 83.00 |
| CD | 3.5 | 2.20 | 4.70 | 250.0 | 3.16 |

**Table 1.4: Seed Fortification and Pelleting in Black Gram**

| Treatment | Number of seeds pod$^{-1}$ | Seed yield (g plant$^{-1}$) | 100 Seed Weight (g) | Seed Recovery (%) | Germination (%) |
|---|---|---|---|---|---|
| Control | 5.70 | 4.80 | 3.60 | 90.00 | 94 |
| Fortified with micro nutrient + pelleting DAP | 6.30 | 5.60 | 3.80 | 94.00 | 96 |
| CD | 0.09 | 0.07 | 0.01 | 0.31 | – |

Mahaeswari (1996)[4] found among the organic pelleting materials tested in Soybean CV Co1, Vermicompost @ 50 gKg$^{-1}$ gave the best effect on germination, peedling growth, dry matter production and vigour index. The next best was the combination of vermicompost and pungam (Derris indica) leaf powder (1:1) @ 40 gkg$^{-1}$.

**Table 1.5: Seed Pelletign with Vermicompost in Soybean**

| Treatment | Germination (%) | Root Length (cm) | Shoot Length (cm) | Dry Matter (mg SL$^{-1}$) | Vigour Index |
|---|---|---|---|---|---|
| Impelleted | 82.0 | 5.10 | 31.5 | 67.0 | 419 |
| Vermicompost | 98.0 | 11.60 | 27.2 | 109.0 | 1136 |
| Vermicompost + pung am leaf powder (1:1) | 92.0 | 11.30 | 26.5 | 93.0 | 1039 |
| CD | 9.2 | 1.20 | 2.9 | 8.7 | 20.0 |

## Maintenance of Purity

To maintain the genetic purity and physical purity of seeds, rouging is to be done form vegetative phase to harvesting phase. The off types and volunteer plants are to be removed as and when they occur in the field based on leaf colour, stem colour, growth status, flower colour, pod colour, seed colour etc. In addition to the off types, the pest affected and mosaic virus affected plants should be removed.

## Irrigation

The crop should be irrigated immediately after sowing and the life irrigation is given on the third day. Subsequently irrigate the crop once in 10-15 days depending upon soil and climatic conditions. The flowering and pod formation stages are critical periods of irrigation. Water stagnation should be avoided at all stages.

## Pre-harvest Sanitation Spray

To avoid bruchid (pulse beetle) infestation in the storage, the pulse crop should be sprayed with endosulfan or malathion 0.07 per cent two times at weekly interval before harvest.

This treatment will minimize the egg laying by bruchid. Sasikala (1994)[5] studied the effect of pre-harvest sanitation spraying of pesticides on seed yield and quality in cowpea CV CO4. the results revealed that pre-harvest spray of endosulfan (0.25%) + Carbendazium (0.1%) two times that is at 30$^{th}$ and 45$^{th}$ after sowing recorded increased number of pods, pod yield, seed yield and seed quality. This treatment also recorded minimum bruchid incidence during storage.

**Table 1.6: Pre-harvest Sanitation Spary in COWPEA CV CO4**

| Treatment | Pod Number/ Plant | Seed Number/ Pod | Pod Yield/ Plant (g) | Seed Yield (g/plant) | Germination (%) |
|---|---|---|---|---|---|
| Control | 6.1 | 14.2 | 14.9 | 10.1 | 87.3 |
| Endosulfon (0.25%) | 8.1 | 13.0 | 17.8 | 11.1 | 93.3 |
| Malathion (0.1%) | 10.1 | 15.3 | 23.0 | 17.2 | 91.7 |
| Carbendazium (0.1%) | 9.0 | 15.7 | 23.2 | 15.9 | 94.7 |
| Endosulfon + Carbendazium | 12.8 | 16.9 | 28.8 | 20.8 | 95.7 |
| Malathion + Carbendaszium | 8.8 | 15.3 | 25.3 | 16.2 | 93.3 |
| CD | 1.01 | NS | 3.40 | 2.50 | 1.91 |

Patrick Jasper (1998)[6] studied the effect of pre-harvest sanitation spray on seed yield and quality in pea. The results showed that the seed yield and quality characters were found to be higher in the plots sprayed with endosulfon 0.1 per cent three times at 10 days intervals before harvesting.

### Harvest

Harvest the pods when they attain the physiological maturity. The pod colour turns straw colour of the crop. Discard the terminal pods, as they invariably contain immature and diseased seeds. The seed moisture content at this stage will be about 15 per cent. Dry the pods to render them just brittle and flail them with pliable bamboo stick to separate the seeds. Rain at the time of harvest may enhance the occurrence of off coloured seeds and result in poor seed quality. These seeds are to be removed.

**Table 1.7: Effect of Seed Treatment in REDGRAM CV CO5**

| Treatment | Seeds Pod $^{-1}$ | Seed Yield g Plan $^{-1}$ | Germination | Vigour Index | Bruchid Infestation |
|---|---|---|---|---|---|
| No spray | 5.5 | 11.3 | 67.0 | 1102.0 | 11.30 |
| Endosulfon | 6.5 | 18.4 | 83.0 | 1197.0 | 1.70 |
| CD | 0.8 | 0.7 | 3.8 | 54.0 | 0.31 |

## Seed Processing

The pods are dried to 12-13 per cent moisture content and then they are threshed and precleaned. The seeds should be size graded using recommended sieve for homogenising the seed lot.

## Seed Treatment

The graded seeds can be further dried to 7-8 per cent moisture content and treated with following materials in the order of preference:

- Thiram or captan @ 2g+ carbaryl @ 200mg kg$^{-1}$ of seed for safe storage.
- Activated clay @ 1 kg 100-1 kg of seeds may be dry dressed for grain cum seed storage use.

## Hybrid Seed Production in Red Gram for COPH 2

The tool employed for production of hybrid seed is by genetic male sterility system (GMS) where the male sterility is maintained in heterozygous stage. Following the test cross principle, these would be fertile and sterile plants in the ratio 1:1 in male sterile production. COPH 1 and COPH 2 are the two red gram hybrids released from TNAU.

## Planting Ratio

For hybrid seed production in COPH 2, a ratio of 4:2 or 6:2 or 4:1 or male sterile; pollen parent is to be adopted depending upon the honey bee activity. If the honey bee activity is above normal, a ratio of 4:1 can be followed. If the honeybee activity is very less a ratio of 4:2 may be adopted. If the activity is moderate adopt 6:2 ratio.

**Isolation Distance**

An isolation distance 200 m for foundation class and 100m for a certified class is to be followed.

**Sowing**

Both the parents are to be sown simultaneously. Sow two rows of pollen parent all around the entire plot. Sowing should be done during Ist fortnight of June or 1st fortnight of December.

**Rogueing**

In male sterile line or female parent,

1. Remove the off type plants.
2. Remove the male fertile plant by examining the colour of the anthers (yellow) at the time of first flower formation. The plants with translucent white anthers (sterile) alone are retained in the female rows. This operation should be completed in 7-10 days interval till completion of flowering by daily visit.
3. Remove the late flowering and early flowering plants.

In male fertile line or pollen parent:

1. Remove all the off type plants.
2. Remove the immature pods set in the plants from time to time to induce continuous flowering and to aware the pollen availability.

**Harvesting**

Collect the pods from the female parent i.e., male sterile parent. This will give the hybrid seeds. Male and female rows can be identified by putting colour bamboo stakes.

Somu (1995)[7] conducted experiments to standardize optimum planting ratio and effect of pickings on seed yield and quality in red gram hybrid ICPH 8. The results revealed that pod set percentage, pod number seed yield per plant and per row were on par up to three rows adjacent to the male row on either side. The hybrid seed yield was significantly higher up to three female rows in either side of male row indicating that the optimum planting ratio for ICPH 8 pigeon pea hybrid seed production is 1: 6 (male: female). The picking wise study revealed that the pod number, pod yield, seed yield and quality showed a decreasing trend from first to third picking.

**Table 1.8: Optimum Planting Ratio for ICPH 8 Hybrid**

| Female Row (R) | Seed Yield (g Plant$^{-1}$) | Seed Yield (q row$^{-1}$) | Germination (%) |
|---|---|---|---|
| $R_1$ | 17.8 | 995 | 89 |
| $R_2$ | 17.4 | 991 | 89 |
| $R_3$ | 16.8 | 987 | 87 |
| $R_4$ | 10.9 | 692 | 86 |
| $R_5$ | 9.0 | 537 | 86 |
| $R_6$ | 4.7 | 294 | 86 |
| $R_7$ | 4.8 | 290 | 87 |
| CD | 1.3 | 20.0 | NS |

Vasantha (1995)[8] studied the better of seed size on seed quality in pigeon hybrid CoH1 and its parents. The results revealed that the pollen and seed parents, ICPL 87109 and MST 21, are large and small seeded genotypes while the hybrid is a medium sized seed. The seed lots of hybrid and its pollen parent can be processed using 12/64 "round perforated sieve while the seed parent with 10/64" sieve in order to get quality seeds with higher germination and vigour.

## Seed Storage and Treatment Techniques in Pulses

Storage is the basic preservation of material for further usage. This occupies special importance in seed since seeds are to be viable at the time of usage for sowing. Seeds undergo irreversible physical, physiological and biochemical deteriorative changes during storage. Seed treatments are the management practices, which can prolong the shelf life of seed by mitigating the deteriorative changes. The seed treatments employed for the said purpose can be broadly classified into pre-storage and mid-storage treatments.

**Table 1.9: Seed Certification Standards for Pulses**

| Field Standards | Foundation Class | Certified Class |
|---|---|---|
| Isolation distance for redgram (m) | 200 | 100 |
| For others(m) | 10 | 5 |
| **Specific requirements** | | |
| Off types | 0.10% | 0.20% |
| *Plants affected by seed borne disease | 0.10% | 0.20% |
| **Seed standards factors** | | |
| Pure seed (minimum) | 98.0% | 98.0% |
| Inert matter (maximum) | 2.0% | 2.05 |
| Other crop seeds (maximum) | 5/kg | 10/kg |
| Weed seeds (maximum) | 5/kg | 10/kg |
| Other distinguishable varieties (maximum) | 5/kg | 10/kg |
| Germination including hard seeds (minimum) | 75% | 75% |
| Moisture (maximum) | 9.0% | 9.0% |
| Containers (maximum) | 8.0% | 8.0% |

* Seed borne diseases are: Ashy stem blight (Macrophomina phaseoli), anthracrose (Colletotrichum lindemuthianum), scochyta blight, cowpea mosaic, Halo blight (Pseudomonas phasiolocola), Bacterial blight (Xanthomonas sapp.)

## PULSES PRODUCTION IN TAMIL NADU

In India black gram is cultivated as major pulse crop under rainfed conditions as rice follow crops. The black gram is cultivated in many parts of the country as an alternative (change) crops to regain the soil fertility[9].

Black gram is one of the important pulses grown in both Kharif and Rabi seasons. It accounts for 41.0 per cent of the total area under pulses during the current year. This crop was extensively grown in Nagapattinam, Thiruvarur, Cuddalore, Toothukudi, Tirunelveli, and Villupuram districts

**Table 1.10: Area, Production and Yield Rate of Pulse Cultivation in Tamil Nadu**

| Pulses | Area (in Hectares) | | | | | Production (in Tonnes) | | | | | Yield Rate (in kg/ha) | | | | |
|---|---|---|---|---|---|---|---|---|---|---|---|---|---|---|---|
| | 2005-06 | 2004-05 | 2003-04 | 2002-03 | 2001-02 | 2005-06 | 2004-05 | 2003-04 | 2002-03 | 2001-02 | 2005-06 | 2004-05 | 2003-04 | 2002-03 | 2001-02 |
| Bengal gram | 5907 | 6420 | 6625 | 6200 | 7010 | 4007 | 3942 | 4349 | 4172 | 4551 | 678 | 614 | 656 | 673 | 649 |
| Red gram | 37769 | 43416 | 44914 | 44127 | 63613 | 20400 | 28979 | 27475 | 24067 | 41420 | 540 | 667 | 612 | 545 | 651 |
| Green gram | 136699 | 154959 | 125690 | 112812 | 128995 | 45881 | 61760 | 53315 | 48053 | 53470 | 336 | 399 | 424 | 426 | 415 |
| Black gram | 215448 | 226364 | 185736 | 196888 | 266123 | 70758 | 82998 | 75920 | 78555 | 104320 | 328 | 367 | 409 | 399 | 392 |
| Horse gram | 60415 | 67513 | 68092 | 81711 | 99980 | 22023 | 20110 | 18240 | 20782 | 42570 | 365 | 298 | 268 | 254 | 426 |
| Other pulses | 68999 | 91578 | 105792 | 121245 | 119682 | 13934 | 18642 | 21757 | 24850 | 24388 | 202 | 204 | 206 | 205 | 204 |
| Total pulses | 525237 | 590250 | 536849 | 562983 | 685403 | 177003 | 216431 | 201056 | 200479 | 270719 | 337 | 367 | 375 | 356 | 395 |
| Total Food grains (A+b) | 33166637 | 3286805 | 2837246 | 2791975 | 3451572 | 6116145 | 6146044 | 4312023 | 4460357 | 7688861 | 1844 | 1870 | 1520 | 1598 | 2228 |

*Source:* Government of Tamil Nadu, department of Economics and Statistics, Seasons and Crop Report 2005-06.

and these districts together accounted for 77.7 per cent of the total area under the crop during 05-06. Green gram is one of the major pulses widely consumed next to Black gram. It is grown in both Kharif and Rabi seasons. The crop was extensively cultivated in Thoothukudi, Thiruvarur, Nagapattinam, and Virudhunagar districts which together accounted for 60.7 per cent of the total area under this crop in the state during 05-06.

Tamil Nadu, which has been lagging behind the rest of the country in the production and productivity of pulses, is making all-out efforts to catch up with others. Since 2001-2002, the State's productivity in pulses has been around 375 kg per hectare. The area coverage has been 5.7 lakh hectares. The production has been of the order of two lakh tonnes annually. However, at the national level, the productivity is nearly 660 kg per hectare and the State's contribution in pulses production is a little more than one per cent. Of the 3316637 ha under food grains, the area under Pulses was 525237 ha. which is 15.8 per cent of the area under food grains.

Annually these crops are grown on an area of 8-9 lakh hectares producing 4.51 lakh tonnes of pulses with a productivity of 454 kg/ha against the national average of 607 kg/ha. Tamil Nadu ranks 10th in terms of area and 11th in terms of production at all India level. Compared to 2009-2010, the State-wide coverage of pulses this year is about one lakh hectares more. At present, it is 8.4 lakh hectares. Eventually, the State will reach about 9.5 lakh hectares.

## PULSES CULTIVATION IN THOOTHUKUDI DISTRICT

Pulses cultivation in Thoothukudi district has witnessed a boom this fiscal, as the productivity and cultivation area exceeded the target multi-fold. While the productivity increased from 400 kg per hectare last fiscal to 700 kg per hectare this financial year, the cultivation area of pulses was 54,394 hectares by the end of the third quarter of the current fiscal itself against an annual target of 25,000 hectares.

Of the 54,394 hectares covered, black gram was raised on 26,479 hectares, green gram on 27,501 hectares, cowpea on 810 hectares, soya bean on 77 hectares and other pulses on 77 hectares, at Ottapidaram, Kayathar, Kovilpatti, Vilathikulam, Pudur and Thoothukudi blocks. The average area covered under pulses in the district during the last 10 financial years stood at 32,744 hectares, with a maximum coverage of 45,543 hectares achieved in 2005-06 fiscal. The average area covered under pulses in the district during the last 10 financial years stood at 32,744 hectares, with a maximum coverage of 45,543 hectares achieved in 2005-06 fiscal.

Accelerated pulses production programme (A3P) has been launched in the district under the aegis of National Food Security Mission (NFSM Pulses 2010-11), a Centrally-sponsored scheme. To increase the yield of pulses, the Department of Agriculture has worked out strategies to implement the programme at Malaipatti village which is attached to Ottapidaram block.

Pulses, which normally grow in Rabi season, is a major crop in Thoothukudi district and 68,000 hectares including all blocks were covered during 2009-10. In the current fiscal, a target of 95,000 ha was fixed under pulse production programme. Normally, the yield of pulse per hectare is between 450 and 500 kilograms in Ottapidaram block but now Department of Agriculture are aiming to achieve between 650 and 700 kilograms per hectare.

## STATEMENT OF THE PROBLEM

India being major pulse growing country in the world, accounting roughly to one third of the total world area under pulses and one fourth of total world production. In India 22.83 million hectare of land is under pulses cultivation with annual production of 11.21 million tonnes. In Tamil Nadu, pulses are cultivated in 8.2 lakh ha with the production of 3.71 lakh metric tonnes. The average productivity of pulses in Tamil Nadu is about 449 kg/ha.

Black gram is the major pulse crop in Tamil Nadu and it is grown in an area of 4.5 lakh ha, and its production is 2.05 lakh tones with a productivity of 461 kg $ha^{-1}$.

In Tamil Nadu, pulses are being cultivated on 0.953 million hectares within the seven million hectares of cultivable lands and this works for 13 per cent as against 29 per cent under rice. The distribution of different pulses to total pulse area is 39 per cent for black gram, 17 per cent for green gram, 15 per cent for red gram, 13 per cent for horse gram, 0.94 per cent for bengalgram and 16 per cent for other pulses. Majority of the black gram area is under rice fallow situation followed by as companion crop in the intercropping system especially under dry land situation. About 55 per cent of total cultivable area (4m ha) is still under dry land, wherein the scopes for the cultivation of crops are in operation.

The production performance of the pulses is of critical importance in improving the efficient use of resources. The cost of production and net returns obtained per unit would determine the profitability of the pulses production. The profitability of an enterprise depends upon the efficient use of the resources in production. The present study is a modest attempt in this regard. This study is an attempt to analyse the economics of pulses cultivation in Thoothukudi district.

## OBJECTIVES OF THE STUDY

The main objective of the study is to analyse the economy of pulses cultivation in Thoothukudi district. The specific objectives of the study are:

1. To analyse the cost and return structure of black and green grams and of small and large farmers producing black and green grams.
2. To identify and analyse the determinants of yield and factors causing yield gap with regard to farmers cultivating two crops of pulses and of small and large farmers group.
3. To estimate and analyse the input demand elasticity's and supply responsiveness of two groups of farmers cultivating black and green grams.

4. To investigate the labour absorption capacity and supply responsiveness of each crop with regard to their own prices and prices of variable inputs and units of fixed inputs.
5. To study the nature and returns to scale for both black and green grams cultivating farmers.

## LIMITATIONS OF THE STUDY

The information on pulses cultivation was collected by survey method through personal interview with the sample farmers, confined to a particular area. Farmers in general were not maintaining detailed accounts on farming and the information on costs and return were elicited from their memory and their experience. Farmers in general are mostly using ancient methods for cultivation. But they are sometimes hesitating to answer regarding the technological oriented questions.

But due efforts and care have been taken by the researcher to get information and data from the respondents and suitable method is adopted for getting some prime information. The researcher has asked several questions to collect the data, according to the circumstances.

Anyhow, due to lack of money, energy and lack of time, the researcher has collected the data from 150 respondents in the study area for the purpose of analysis and discussion.

## CHAPTER SCHEME

The report of the present study *"Economic Efficiency in Pulses Cultivation"* has been organised and presented in eight chapters.

*Chapter I* introduces the subject and deals with the importance of pulses, pulses cultivation in India and Tamil Nadu, statement of the problem, objectives of the study, limitations of the study and chapter scheme.

*Chapter II* reviews the earlier studies relating to the cost of production, yield gap and yield constraints and profit function approach and various concepts used in the study.

*Chapter III* describes the methodology which includes the choice of the study area, sample design, collection of data, period of study, methods of analysis and tools of analysis and measurement of variables. Further, the profile of the study area is also presented in this chapter.

*Chapter IV* analyses the characteristics of sample farmers, the cost and returns structure of pulses cultivation.

*Chapter V* examines the determinants of yield, yield gap and yield constraints.

*Chapter VI* discusses input demand elasticity's, supply responsiveness and labour absorption in pulses cultivation.

*Chapter VII* presents a summary of the findings, the results arrived at and the suggestions made in the context of the research findings.

## REFERENCES


1. Maheswari R (1996), Seed Production Technology in Soybean under Rice Fallow and Methods to Control Seed Detenoration in Soybean CV Col. (Glycine max L) Merrill, M.Sc., (Agri). Thesis, Tamil Nadu Agricultural University, Coimbatore.
2. Palanisamy, V. and K. Jayaseelan, (1998), Effect of Pre-sowing Seed Treatments on Seed Quality in Redgram, MAJ 85 (10-12), pp. 612-614.
3. Vijaya J. and A.S. Ponnusamy, (1998), Studies on Seed Fortification and Pelloting in Blackgram, Madurai Agricultural Journal, (10-12), pp. 549-552.
4. Ibid., p. 12.
5. Sasikala, K. 1994, Studies on the Influence of Pre-harvest Spraying of Pesticides on Seed Yield and Quality in Cowpea CV Co. 4, M.Sc., Agri Thesis, TNAU, Coimbatore.
6. Patrick Jasper (1998) Studies on Seed Production and Storage Aspects of Pea (Pisum Sativum L.) M.Sc. Agri. Thesis TNAU, Coimbatore.
7. Somu, G. (1995), Studies on Certain Aspects of Seed Production in Pigeon Pea (Cajanus Cajan (L) Millsp), Hybrid ICPH 8 M.Sc., (Agri) Thesis, TNAU, Coimbatore.
8. Vasantha, R. (1995), Certain seed Technological Studies in the Piegon pea (Cajanus Cajan (L), millsp) Hybrid Co H1 and its parental lines M.Sc., (Agri), Thesis TNAU, Coimbatore.
9. GoI (2009), Data Base on Indian Agriculture, Department of Agriculture and Cooperation, http;dacnet.nic.in.

# CHAPTER 2

# Review of Literature and Concepts

This chapter is devoted to review the literature related to the present study. For any research, a review of the past studies related to the subject is useful in several ways. It helps in defining concepts and operational definitions, in formulating testable hypotheses, specifying test conditions, choice of analytical tools as empirical models and in evaluating the findings of the research in the light of the results of earlier studies so as to explain the differences if any.

## REVIEW OF LITERATURE

For better exposition, the review has been organised under the following heads:

1. Studies relating to Cost and Production
2. Studies relating to Yield Gap and Yield Constraints and
3. Studies relating to Profit Function Approach
4. Studies relating to Pulses

### Studies Relating to Cost of Production

In agriculture, cost of production refers to the expenditure incurred by the farmers on the various inputs (operational and fixed) to obtain the final produce. The relationship between cost and income is of vital importance. In agriculture, costs of farming may be classified under two major heads namely, fixed cost and variable or operational costs. Fixed costs include depreciation, taxes, rent, interest, insurance and premium. It results from past commitments of cost already sunk. It is contrast over time and does not vary with the changes in output. It exists even in the absence of cultivation. Variable cost includes input like seeds, labour cost, manures and pesticides, tractor fuel and livestock fuel. It varies with the changes in the level of output. It does not exist in the absence of cultivation. It is an important factor which determines how much and what is to be produced. Fixed cost is important in making decisions on the amount to be produced and different practices to be adopted. In the long run, all costs become variable costs.

In the short run, it is profitable for a farmer to produce as long as gross income in greater than or covers the variable cost. But in the long run, the return must cover the total cost, comprising of both variable cost and fixed cost.

In agricultural operations, the farm cost of production refers to the expenses incurred on the various inputs (both operational and fixed) to obtain the final produce. The cost of production consists of two parts, namely fixed cost and variable or operational cost. In farm management studies, Shukla[1] has categorised cost into Cost A1, Cost A2, Cost B and Cost C. Cost A1 includes the cost of seeds, manures and fertilisers, plant protection, livestock expenses, hired human labour, irrigation charges, land revenue, interest on working capital, depreciation of fixed assets and miscellaneous expenses. Cost A2 covers Cost A1 plus rent paid for leased in land. Cost B includes Cost A2 plus rental value of owned land plus interest on fixed capital minus land revenue on owned land. Cost C includes Cost B plus imputed value of family labour.

Rajagopalan[2] et al., in their study on the cost of production of crops in Tamil Nadu during the year 1978.

**Cost A**

*(i)* Value of human labour including family labour
*(ii)* Value of bullock labour
*(iii)* Value of machinery charges
*(iv)* Value of seed
*(v)* Value of insecticides
*(vi)* Value of manures and fertilizers
*(vii)* Cost of irrigation and
*(viii)* Interest on working capital

**Cost C**

Cost A plus rent (including actual rent paid by the tenant or rental value of owned land) interest on fixed capital, land revenue, cesses, taxes and depreciation of implements and machinery.

The cost individually includes.

**(i) Cost A1:**

1. Value of hired labour (permanent and casual)
2. Value of owned bullock labour
3. Value of hired bullock labour
4. Value of owned machinery
5. Hired machinery charges
6. Value of fertilizers
7. Value of manure (owned and purchased)
8. Value of seed (with farm produced and purchased)
9. Value of insecticides and pesticides
10. Irrigation charges (both owned and hired machineries)
11. Canal water charges
12. Land revenue, cesses and other taxes
13. Depreciation on farm implements (both bullock drawn and used by human labour)
14. Depreciation on farm building, farm machinery and irrigation structure.

15. Interest on working capital and
16. Miscellaneous expenses (artisans, so far and repairs to small farm implements)

**(ii) Cost A2**

It includes Cost A1 and

17. Rent paid for leased in land

**(iii) Cost B**

It includes Cost A2 and

18. Imputed rental value of owned land (less land revenue paid there upon) and
19. Imputed interest on fixed capital (excluding land).

**(iv) Cost C**

It includes Cost B and

20. Imputed value of family labour.

When a farmer is the owner and has contributed land and other resources, he incurs Cost A1. In case all the land is leased in and rent has to be paid, Cost A2 is incurred. It is also known as tenant cost. In addition to it if the imputed interest is paid on owned fixed capital, Cost B is incurred. Cost C is incurred if the imputed cost of family labour is also considered. Cost C is a very comprehensive cost.

In a study conducted by Tamil Nadu Agricultural University, Coimbatore, on the cost of production of mango in Tamil Nadu, Cost A and Cost C alone were used.[3]

They include the following cost components.

**(i) Cost A:**

1. Value of human labour including family labour;
2. Value of bullock labour;
3. Value of machinery charges;
4. Value of seed;
5. Value of insecticides;
6. Value of manure and fertilizer;
7. Value of irrigation; and

8. Investment on working capital.

**(ii) Cost C:**

Cost A plus rent (includes actual rent paid by the tenant or rental value of owned land) plus interest on fixed capital including land plus land revenue, cesses and taxes plus depreciation of implements and machinery.

Cost A was computed from Cost C, on the assumption that Cost A accounted for 70 per cent of the Cost C. But the assumption is highly arbitrary.

In the survey of cost of production of raw cotton conducted by the International Cotton Advisory Committee, Memphis, U.S.A., costs were divided into direct cost and indirect cost.[4] Direct cost was the cost associated with physical production. It included on-farm production and harvesting cost and off-farm cost like transportation and gearing charges. Indirect or overhead cost included management and land cost. These two kinds of costs formed the gross cost for producing seed cotton.

In the present study, Cost A (operational cost) and Cost C (fixed cost) were conducted to arrive at the cost and return structure of paddy cultivation in the study area. The following items formed the components of the two costs:

**(i) Cost A:**

1. Human labour
2. Bullock labour
3. Chemical fertilizer
4. Pesticides
5. Seed cost
6. Farm manures
7. Cost of irrigation and
8. Interest on working capital.

**(ii) Cost C:**

1. Rent; and
2. Interest on fixed capital, land revenue, cesses and taxes, depreciation of implements and machinery.

David Groenfeldt[5] in his study stated that paddy cultivation forms the basis of traditional Southeast Asian societies and the livelihoods of the people who comprise those societies. Historically speaking, paddy cultivation has always (at least for several millennia) been multi-functional – providing not only the raw material for subsistence and trade, but also serving as the central focus for family and community life as well as spiritual and religious expression. While times have certainly changed, this paper suggests that the multi-functional nature of paddy cultivation continues to be important, and that our concept of rural "livelihood" should incorporate these cultural dimensions.

Kumar et al.,[6] in their study on "Technical Efficiency of Rice Farms under Irrigated Conditions of North West Himalayan Region – A Non-Parametric Approach" stated that hill agriculture is practiced under tough conditions because of its unique character. The hill and mountain ecosystem is unique because of topographical features and climatic variations along the gradient. In general, hills receive 750 to 1250 mm precipitation; however, only about 10 per cent of the area is under irrigation in Uttaranchal hills that too confined to the lower valleys. Sub-optimal hydro-thermal regimes and shallow soil depths thwart further extension of cultivated land. Small and scattered land holdings and limited land use is also the main feature of hill agriculture. Therefore, the food produced is not sufficient to sustain for the whole year. These biophysical and socio-economic constraints result in low technical efficiency as well as discourage farmers to bear the risk. In this context increasing technical efficiency assumes significance. Improving efficiency levels under these conditions is a big challenge for farmers in the NWH region. Rice being the most important staple food in NWH region, improvement in efficiency levels is one of the major means of sustaining their staple food production and thereby ensuring food security.

This study was taken up to determine the efficiency of rice cultivation under irrigated conditions in NWH region. Moreover, the study also explores the possibility, if any, the difference in technical efficiency levels between the local and improved technology (i.e., variety) in rice growing farms. The factors associated with inefficiency are also analysed.

The overall technical efficiency in the case of improved rice growing farms is higher than that of rice farms growing local varieties. The results also indicate that in case of local rice growing farms, the scale inefficiency contributes more to the overall technical inefficiency. From the policy point of view, increasing the share of rice cultivation under irrigated situation in the total farm area can bring about improvement in the overall technical efficiency. With regard to farms growing improved rice varieties, pure technical inefficiency makes the greatest contribution to the overall inefficiency. By emulating the best practices of relevant efficient farms, less efficient farms growing improved rice varieties can eliminate pure technical inefficiency under irrigated conditions.

A. Suresh and T.R. Keshava Reddy[7] in their study on "Resource-use efficiency of Paddy Cultivation in Peechi Command Area of Thrissur District of Kerala: An Economic Analysis" undertaken in the Peechi Command Area of Thrissur district in the Kerala state, has examined the resource productivity and allocate as well as the technical efficiency of paddy production. The study has used the primary data collected from 71 rice farmers of the command area using the stratified random sampling. The cost of cultivation of paddy in the command area has been found as Rs 21603/ha, resulting in a BC ratio of 1.34. The elasticity coefficients for chemical fertilizers, farmyard manure and human labour have been observed significant and positive. The allocate efficiency has indicated that marginal return per one rupee increase under these heads would be Rs 2.83, Rs 1.57 and Rs 1.17, respectively. The average technical efficiency of the paddy farmers in the command area has been found as 66.8 per cent. Education of the farmer and supplementary irrigation provided during the water-stress days have been identified as the factors which could enhance the technical efficiency. The study has called for an equitable distribution of canal water and enhanced extension services for resource management in the area.

Ansari and Ismail[8] in their investigations were conducted at the farms of Uttar Pradesh Bhumi Sudhar Nigam at Shivri, Lucknow during the Kharif season in 1998-99 to assess the impact of organic amendment vermicompost in comparison to chemical fertilisers on paddy (variety-Sarju-52) in sodic soil and in relation to soil fertility, yield parameters and economics. Results indicated an increase in soil organic matter from 0.38 to 0.96 per cent, organic carbon from 0.22 to 0.56 per cent, available nitrogen (N) from 499.52 to 1245.44 kg / ha, carbonate ions from 0.20 to 0.23 meq/100 g of soil, calcium ions from 0.89 to 1.09 meq/100 g of soil and decrease in pH from 8.74 to 8.25, electric conductivity (EC) from 0.86 to 0.69 dSm-1, sodium ions from 11.85 to 1.47 meq/100 g of soil and exchangeable sodium percentage (ESP) from 67.51 to 57.42, suggesting qualitative improvement of soil, in the plots amended with vermicompost. Paddy yield of 4975 kg/ha was recorded from plots amended with vermicompost while 4900 kg/ha, from plots amended with chemical fertilizers, as control. Cost benefit ratio was found to be 1:1.5 for cultivation of paddy using vermitech where as in case of chemical fertilisers, it was 1:1.06 suggesting that by the application of vermicompost in paddy, the cost of production could be reduced without compromising on harvest.

Bassvaraja et al.,[9] in their research notes stated that the quantitative analysis of agricultural production systems has become an important step in the formulation of agricultural policy. A number of empirical studies have attempted to investigate producer responsiveness to product and input price changes, to estimate economies of scale, to assess the relative efficiency, and to measure the impact of technological change. In particular, there has been a considerable amount of theoretical and applied econometric research on the measurement of the impact of technological change. As knowledge of new and more efficient methods of production (cultivation in agriculture) become available, technology changes. The adoption of new or improved method of production/cultivation can shift the production function. In other words, production can be increased with new technology by using same quantities of resources that were used in old technology or alternatively, the production level in old technology can be attained with new technology by using fewer quantities of inputs. The recent breakthrough in rice cultivation known as System of Rice Intensification (SRI) method is one such case which may be considered as disembodied technology.

The study was based on the input-output data obtained from sample paddy growing farmers in Andhra Pradesh selected through multi-stage sampling design. At the first stage, four major paddy growing districts, namely Prakasam, East Godavari, West Godavari and Guntur districts following both traditional and SRI methods of rice cultivation were purposively selected. From each district, three major paddy growing mandals following both the methods of rice cultivation were selected purposively at the second stage. Then at the third stage, four major paddy growing villages following both methods were purposively chosen from each mandal. In the final stage, ten farmers were randomly selected from each village such that they included five farmers in SRI method and five farmers in traditional method of rice cultivation. Thus, 480 farmers (240 farmers growing paddy by traditional method and 240 farmers growing it by SRI method) spread over four districts of Andhra Pradesh were interviewed during kharif season of 2005-06. The data on various inputs used in paddy cultivation like chemical fertilizers, plant protection chemicals, seed materials and human labour, and cultivation practices such as land preparation, transplanting, irrigation, inter-cultivation and harvesting along with labour requirement for these operations were collected from the sample farmers.

The findings of this study demonstrate the superiority of SRI in terms of yield and returns advantage. However, it is worth mentioning here that the actual adoption rate of SRI among paddy growers is very low, which appears to be a puzzle given the encouraging performance of the new technology. There are several reasons for this kind of poor response of farmers to SRI method. First, the farmers, particularly in the head reaches of command areas, where paddy is grown extensively, have not fully realised the importance of water in view of market and policy failure in pricing the resource appropriately; second, intensive care particularly during transplanting of seedlings and higher weed infestation demands more labour and hence farmers in labour scarce areas are hesitant to adopt SRI; third, only soils with good drainage facility and low clay content are suitable for SRI cultivation and finally, there is not enough awareness among farmers about its superiority.

M. Shivamurthy et al.,[10] in their study stated that rice growing situations prevailing in different regions of India largely determine the system of rice cultivation. The two principle systems of cultivation in Karnataka are dry and wet. The dry system of cultivation is mainly confined to tracks which depend on rains only. Upland rice, which is predominantly cultivated in the arid and semi- arid zones, has noticed a gradual decline in its area and quantum of production in the recent years. The factors attributing to this decline are lack of suitable high yielding varieties and drought resistant varieties, decline in the relative profitability of rice cultivation and shifting from food crops to cash crops etc.,. The present study was conducted to identify the constraints faced by farmers cultivating rain fed paddy in Eastern Dry Zone of Karnataka.

The study was conducted in Bangalore Rural, Tumkur and Kolar districts under Eastern Dry Zone of Karnataka State during 2005. Out of 24 taluks belongs to these three districts, six taluks (Kanakapura, Channapatna, Tumkur, Gubbi, Kolar and Bangarpet) were selected based on the highest area under paddy cultivation. From among these six taluks, 25 villages were selected randomly. In each of the 25 so selected villages, a list of farmers growing rain fed paddy during 2003- 04 *kharif* season was prepared. From each village four rain fed paddy growers were selected by adopting simple random sampling technique. Thus, 100 rainfed paddy growing farmers spread over 25 villages were selected for the study. The data was collected from 100 rainfed paddy growing farmers with the help of a pre-structured interview schedule.

**Studies Relating to Yield Gap and Yield Constraints**

There are two common ways of defining the concept of yield gap; First, directly comparing the experiment station yield to the yield at farm; Second, comparing yield of the best farm with that of the average on the poorest farm.[11] Thus, yield gap may be classified into two kinds - Yield gap I and Yield gap II. The Yield Gap I represent the difference between the experiment station yield and potential farm yield. Yield Gap II corresponds to the potential farm yield and actual farm yield. The maximum yield obtainable from a variety under particular situation is called 'potential yield', which the average yield attained under farm condition is known as 'actual yield'.

Yield gap analysis becomes instrumental in measuring the magnitude of gap in the yields and in identification of constraints responsible for it. It is not proper to consider Yield Gap I in a study, as experiment station rarely encounters the constraints experienced by the farmers. Such estimates would be biased and larger than what it is actually under the farmer's condition.[12] Hence, Yield Gap II has been examined in the study. It was defined as the difference between the highest yield obtained by the most efficient farmer in the sample and the average level of yield achieved under farmer's condition.

Davidson and Martin[13] in their study, "The Relationship between Yields on Farm and in Experiments Station" was observed to vary according to the cultivation season. During good years, the yield at experiment station was found to increase more rapidly than the yield on farm within the same district. This was mainly because the farmers were more interested in measuring their profit by limiting their input investments, while the experimenters only aimed at measuring yield and had no cost restraints.

Mokheyi[14] in his study estimated the yield gap ratios in rice production during kharif season in the year 1975-76 the deserved farmers technical competence to be high when the gap ratio was low and vice versa. High yield gap was reported in states like Bihar and Orissa. This was attributed to the fact that while the demonstration plots were situated in irrigated areas, rice at the farmer was generally produced under rainfed conditions.

Tripathy[15] in his study, "A Study of Technological Crop in Adoption of New Rice Technology in Coastal Orissa and Constraints Responsible in the same", concluded that, about 17 per cent of the gap in the yield was caused by technology gap. The different package of practices individually accounts for the technological gaps. There are 20.34 per cent, 17.92 per cent and 12.37 per cent of the gaps which were caused by water management, disease and pest control, and nitrogen application respectively. Nearly 20 per cent of the gap was due to the ecological factors like temperature, soil, rainfall and sunshine intensity.

Gomez[16] defined the factors responsible for yield gap constraints. Yield Gap I was hypothesised to be caused by other environmental differences between experiment station and farmer's field or by non-transfer of technology. Yield Gap II was caused by biological and socio-economic constraints. Biological constraints referred to the uncontrollable natural factors and socio-economic constraints to the social and economic factors that prevented the farmers from using the recommended technology. The author developed the conceptual model of yield gap. The farmer corresponded to the difference between experiment station yield and potential farm yield and the latter corresponded to the difference between the potential farm yield and actual farm yield.

David Rajasekar[17] studied the relationship between yield gap and the associated input gaps by fitting linear yield gap functions for paddy, irrigated cholam and irrigated cumbu separately and log linear yield gap function for irrigated groundnut. In the case of paddy, the co-efficient of nitrogen gap, human labour gap and technology index were significant which indicated that the yield gap between demonstration plots and farm holdings would be bridged physically by increasing the inputs such as labour, nitrogen and technology level in the sample farm. In the case of groundnut, the coefficient of phosphorous gap, potash gap and pesticides gap was significant. So, the economic optima derived revealed that there existed potentialities for increasing the groundnut yield by bridging the gaps in phosphorous, potash and pesticides.

Suryawanshri and Gaikward[18] in their study found that there was a wide gap in yield when new technology was adopted. The yield was 2.12 quintals/ha. under traditional method of cultivation but it was 3.42 quintals/ha. when there was a partial adoption of technology. It was 7.02 quintals/ha. when it was fully adopted as in demonstration plot. Multiple regression analysis showed that not only sowing had increased yield of jowar but also contributed to increase productivity of the resource. Recommended varieties, fertilizers and timely sowing were found to be important ways to reduce the yield gap.

Chandrasekaran[19] in his study examined the relationship between yield gap and the associated input gap by fitting a linear function. The co-efficient of gap is nitrogen, phosphorous and potash were significant which included that the yield gap between demonstration plots and the farm holdings could be bridged by increasing the input such as nitrogen, phosphorous and potash in the sample farm. He found that the marginal value product of nitrogen, phosphorus and potash was higher than the marginal cost of the respective and be concluded that even at the existing product and factor prices, the yield gap could be reduced.

Fale et al[20]., in their study "An Economic Analysis of Yield Gap in Rice in Ratnagiri District" argued that yield obtained at the experimental station cannot be advanced on farm because of differences in environment, input use and management. Therefore, they defined yield gap on the difference between the potential yield, that is, yield obtained in demonstration plots and the actual farm yields. They defined potential yield that could be obtained in farmer's field by adopting improved technology. They observed that the gap between yields, in experimental station and those obtained in national demonstration plots (Gap 1) was quite misnomer (2 q/ha. or 3.82 per cent). However, the gap between potential yield and the actual yield on farmers fields was very wide (that is, 27 q/ha. or 52 per cent). There existed differences in utilisation of improved inputs such as fertilizer and labour. Higher level of input was used on national demonstration plots as compared to farmer level.

Flinn and Ali[21] studied the yield gap in two villages of Gujranwala district, Pakistan, using data collected from a random sample 115 farmers. The mean yield of Basmala variety was found to be 1.8 tonnes per hectare over the sampled farm during 198.2 rice crop. The yield of rice in the study ranged from 0.6 to 3.0 tonnes per hectare. Thus, a yield gap of over one tonne per hectare was identified between the average and the highest farm yield. This suggested that given current technology, there were opportunities for increasing rice yields in the study area.

Yadav and Gangwar[22] in their study, "Rice Production and Constraints in Bihar State" stated that, high yielding variety rice yield was 35.56 quintals per hectare which was about 160 per cent higher than that of local varieties. Yield gap between potential farm yield and the actual realised yield was quite high indicating factor potential for increase in production of rice in state. The reason for this yield gap was only the partial adoption of new technologies. The author remarked that there was a need to strengthen the extension and input supply services in Bihar immediately.

Subramaniyan and Nirmala[23] in their study "Yield Gap Analysis in Rice Cultivation", analysed the yield gap among IR 20 and CO 37 rice cultivation in Gokilapuram village of Madurai district for khariff 1986. Yield gap under the former variety (3.54 qtls per acre) worked out to be greater than that under the latter (2.81 qtl per acre). Further, Garretts ranking technique was used to identify the important constraints to potential yield in the study area. The main constraints observed were shortage, insects, credit, tradition, weeds and non-availability of seeds.

Lakshmanan[24] in his study revealed that the extent of yield gap in groundnut varied from 20.84 per cent in wet zone area to 29.05 per cent in dry zone. The gap was 26.41 per cent and 22.79 per cent in the case of small and big farmers respectively. The reason for the variation was due to low fertilizer dose, irrigation and low perception of attributes.

**Yield Constraints**

The factors that prevent farmers from achieving the potential yield under farmer condition are known as 'yield constraints'.

There are three kinds of constraints[25], which cause yield gap. They are:

1. environmental constraint;
2. biological constraints; and
3. socio-economic constraints.

Environmental constraints are caused by:

1. environmental difference; and
2. non-transferable technology.

Experiment stations are usually located in places ideal for farming, whereas the same is not true for farmer's field. Moreover, there are hardly any cost output constraints at these centres, while farmers often encounter such problems at farm level. Above all, some of the technologies adopted at the experiment station may not be transferable to a farmer's field. These constraints cause Yield Gap I. Biological constraints include:

1. variety;
2. weeds;
3. diseases and insects;
4. problem soil;
5. irrigation facilities; and
6. soil fertility.

By and large, these constraints arise from the non-application of the required inputs. Experiment station may not face such problems, while farmers often face them at the farm level.

Socio-economic constraints arise from:

1. costs and returns;
2. credit problems;
3. tradition and attitudes;
4. knowledge; and
5. input availability of institutional facilities.

It is the outcome of these constraints which prevent the farmers from adopting the technology as recommended. A farmer may consider the economic viability of following the new technology in terms of its cost and returns. Some farmers may not like to give up their traditional practices. Moreover, some aspects of the technology may not be understood by them. It also results from lack of institutional facilities like non-availability of inputs and credits. Biological and socio-economic constraints together contribute towards Yield Gap II.

**Studies Relating to Profit Function Approach**

Most of the empirical studies discussed in the previous section made use of the Cobb- Douglas production function to evaluate the economic efficiency of the farmers. According to Lau and Yotopoulas[26], production function approach is not suited to examine the allocative efficiency of farmers, because the prices are not incorporated as exogenous variables nor does the approach allow for different groups of farmers having different endowments of factor inputs.[27] To avoid limitations Lau and Yotopoulos[28] applied the profit function concept to the analysis of relative efficiency of Indian agriculture. They have developed an operation model to measure and compare economic efficiency of farmers on the basis of the following assumptions:

1. Farms are profit maximizing;
2. Farmers are price takers in both product and factor markets; and

3. The production function, which underlies the profit function, is concave in variable inputs.

In the Cobb-Douglas production function in the variable inputs with n fixed inputs, the normalized restricted profit function[29] is given by

$$\log n^{*} = \log A^{*} + \sum_{i=1}^{m} {}^{*}\log p_i + \sum_{i=1}^{n} rj \log zj$$

where

$n^{*}$ = Normalised restricted profit

$A^{*}$ = Normalised shift parameter

$p_i$ = Normalised prices of inputs in the production process

$z_j$ = Fixed inputs

The levels of variable inputs can be derived from the above equation by differentiating the normalised restricted profit function with respect to the normalised price for that factor by using Sheppard's Lemma.[30] From the equation the variable input demands function[31] are derived as

$$\frac{-p_i x_i}{n^{*}} = \beta_1^{*}$$

Where $X_i$ = levels of variable inputs

$i = 1 \ldots\ldots m$

The above equations are to be estimated jointly by using Zellners[32] seemingly unrelated regression with an assumption of additive error with zero expectation and finite variance for each of the two equations. The hypothesis of equal relative economic efficiency of two different farms can be tested by using dummy variable in the normalised restricted profit function and examining whether its value is equal to zero.

Kalirajan and Flinn[33] studied allocative efficiency and supply response in irrigated rice production through profit function. The study was confined to two varieties of rice in the kharif reason in Coimbatore district, Tamil Nadu. The data used were drawn from a larger intensive survey conducted from May 1977 to April 1978. They chose 41 farmers for Exotic Modern Variety (EMV) at random. They estimated Lau-Yolopoulus profit function along with input demand equation by using the restricted Aitten's estimation, imposing the conditions that the co-efficient of variable input are equal in both profit and relevant factor demand equation. The interest terms of the normalised profit function indicated similar technical efficiency of the EMV and LBV producers. The sum of the elasticities of fixed factors (land and capital) indicated that constant returns to scale prevail in both cases.

The output responses to changing rice price were positive, significant and greater than one. This indicated that the farmers in the study area were responsive to changes in rice price. Besides this, farmers supply response for rice was sensitive to changes in the prices of rice, fertilizer and labour wages.

Junakar[34] tested the joint hypothesis of profit maximising behaviour and competitive behaviours of Indian farmers. The study was based on cross sections data pertaining to paddy growing farmers of Thanjavur district in Tamil Nadu, for 1969-70. He estimated Lau-Yotopoulas profit function along with that variable input demand equation by Zellner's Seemingly Unrelated Regression and tested the restriction implied by theory. Quite contrary to the earlier findings of other studies, assuming competitive conditions, he found that Indian farmers were not profit maximizers. He argued that small and large farmers in India did not operate in the same credit or labour markets, and therefore, they were not competitive. Hence, he emphasised the need for further research to explain the behaviour of farmers in poor countries.

Abhi, Kumar and Mathur[35] derived indirect production elasticities for three varieties of cotton (Desi cotton, American cotton and Hybrid cotton) using Lau -Yotopoulus profit function along with variable input demand equation relating to labour. They utilized farm level primary data from Akola district in Maharashtra state, for the year 1979-80, for 200 farmers growing three varieties of cotton. They estimated profit equation along with input demand (labour) equation jointly by using Zellner's Seemingly Unrelated Regression. The study showed that the share of land in cotton production was the maximum for all varieties of cotton, ranging from 0.42 for Desi cotton to 0.54 for American and Hybrid cotton. The share of labour decreased substantially as one moved from 'old' to 'new' technology. The share of capital in Hybrid cotton technology was biased towards land and capital, and was against labour.

Kalirajan[36] studied the economic efficiency of farmer groups (small and large) using Lau-Yotopoulas profit function along with four variable input demand equations relating to labour, chemical fertilizer, pesticides and bullock pair. For the empirical estimation of profit and variable factor demand function a random sample of seventy farmers (35 farmers each) growing HYV. IR 20 in rabi (winter) reason 1977-78 was selected from a progressive village in Coimbatore district, Tamil Nadu.

To test the equality of different efficiencies (economic, price and technical) between the two farmer groups, he estimated the profit function along with demand functions, jointly by using Aitken's genratlised least squares through the Lagragian Multiplier. This way of estimating profit and factor demand functions is different from the method of Lau and Yolopoulus. The advantage of working with this method is that it is possible to identify which elasticities estimated from the factor demand equations differ from those of the profit functions. It helps policy makers to identify which of the factors effect farmer decision is making. The major findings of this study were:

1. There was equal relative economic efficiency is the cultivation of IR 20 in rabi season between small and large farm groups.

2. There were equal differences between price efficiency parameters of small and large farm groups; and
3. The null hypothesis of equal relative technical efficiency between small and large farm groups could not be rejected.

These findings indicate that given the same acres to input and equal terms, small farmers would respond to economic opportunities in the same way as large farmers. However, in order to achieve this, special institutional arrangements may be necessary to ensure equal access for small farmers to inputs.

The methodology adopted to test the difference in various relative efficiencies was as follows:

**(i) Test for Equal Relative Economic Efficiency:**

$H_0 : \delta^*_L = 0$

If this hypothesis is rejected at appropriate level of significance (they used 10 per cent level). One may infer that the groups of farms (small and large) differ with regard to economic efficiency.

**(ii) Test for Equal Relative Price Efficiency:**

$H_0 : \propto_1^{*L} = \propto_1^{*S}$

If this hypothesis is accepted at appropriate level of significance, one can accept that the two groups of farms (small and large) do not have different price efficiency parameters that is they both succeed to the same degree in maximising profit.

**(iii) Test of Equal Relative Technical and Price Efficiency:**

$H_0 : \delta^*_L = 0$

$H_0 : \propto_1^{*L} = \propto_1^{*S}$

If this hypothesis is accepted at appropriate level of significance, one can infer that the two groups of farms (small and large) are equal in technical and price efficiency, not otherwise. If hypothesis *(i)* is rejected then the rejection of this hypothesis *(ii)* may be anticipated.

**(iv) Test for Absolute Price Efficiency of Small Farms:**

$H_0 : \propto_1^{*L} = \propto_1^{*S}$

If this hypothesis is accepted at appropriate level of significance, one can say that small farms have maximized profits.

**(v) Test for Absolute Price Efficiency of Large Farms:**

$H_0 : \propto_1^{*L} = \propto_1^{*S}$

If this hypothesis is not rejected at appropriate level of significance, one can infer that large farms have maximised profits.

The major finding of their study (Lau and Yotopoulus 1973) was that the test of relative economic efficiency was in favour of small farms. Given the fixed inputs (land and fixed capital), and within the ranges of the observed prices of output and variable input, small farms have higher actual profits. They found that this difference was not due to superior price efficiency but due to superior technical the efficiency of constant returns to scale in Indian agriculture. Therefore, one cannot argue for consolidation of small farms on the grounds of economies of scale.

While using this model in empirical context one has to note the following points:

(i) The estimates of parameter $\propto_1^{*L}$, $\propto_1^{*S}$, $\log A_*^S$ $\beta_1^*$, $\beta_2^*$ etc are all group level estimates. Therefore, the estimates at the farm level cannot be obtained from them.

Models to be used in the Present Study

Sampath[37] has discussed the unreliability of conventional production function approach to evaluate the economic efficiency of farmers due to the elastic assumptions and the econometric problems involved in the estimation of the elasticity parameters.

He has suggested linear programming as an alternative approach to measure and compare the economic efficiency of the multi product farm. But the linear programming approach is not advantageous and it is inappropriate for a single crop study.[38] The next alternative approach to measure and evaluate the economic efficiency of farmers is the profit function approach. The profit function presents itself as a superior alternative to the production function for the following main reasons.

1. The normalised restricted profit function and input demand function are functions of predetermined variables and estimation of such function avoids possible simultaneous equation bias.[39]
2. The hypothesis concerning economic efficiency can be tested directly from profit function without having allocative error function.
3. The profit function approach takes into account differences in technical efficiency, allocative efficiency and efficiency in prices and also permits determination of relative economic efficiency of the different group of farms.[40]

In order to measure and examine the relative economic efficiency and its component of technical efficiency and price efficiency, the profit function approach seems to be an ideal tool.[41]

Hence, in the present study, profit function and input demand functions with and without restrictions have to be estimated for fulfilling the objectives.

**Studies Relating to Pulses**

Mr. K.Seerangan Addl.Director (inputs) in pulses seminar organised at National pulses research centre discusses the various issues related to growth and adoption of technologies to assess the growth rate and to improve[42].

Prof. Dr. S. Kanniayan vice Chancellor, Tamilnadu Agricultural University pointed out that the growth rate is affected by various factors such as moisture conditions, lack of proper seed storage facilities and growing lands such as marginal lands, Irrigation prone areas, fertile lands occupied for other purpose etc.

He says that growth rate of 20 per cent is only possible under irrigation prone and free from pests and diseases[43].

Economic growth depends upon its natural resources, human resources capital, enterprise, technology etc.

Gourou explains about the tropical soils and weeds Mechanization to the increase of Growth rate and helping the increase of yield by the effective use of fertilizers[44].

Dr. Subramanian K.V and vasanthi reveals that the growth rate is usually estimated on the basis of different functional forms. Equating method has been used even if the growth rate is accelerating or decelerating, they used semi log functions to find the compound growth rates of Area, production and productivity for six crops, namely paddy, seeds, pulses, vegetables, wheat, maize. They used time series data from 1961 to 1978 and also divided this into two sub-periods, i.e. 1961-1969 and 1970-1978.

They concluded that growth rates in period II (1970-78) were generally higher than those of period I (1961-1969) which indicated the impact of green revolution on all the crops[45].

Dr. G. Subramanian computed simple annual growth rates of area, production and products of various pulses. He also describes the state-wise production and Growth rate of black gram and other pulses. The growth rate of black gram in Tamilnadu is 1.43 per cent after green revolution[46].

Dr. Masood Ali Director and Dr. Shivkumar principal scientist of head of improvement division Indian Institute of Pulses Research Kanpur, in a survey of Indian agriculture 2007 says that Domestic production of pulses is 14.94 million tonnes in 2003-04 had declined to 13.38 million tonnes in 2004-05 and to 13.11 million tonnes in 2005-06. The growth rate is decreased 0.56 per cent from 2003-04 to 2005-06; whereas in 2005-06 it is declined as 1.83 per cent[47].

They concluded that compound growth rate of area under pulses cultivation. Production and productivity has been increases due to increase in the yield per unit area[48].

Sharma and Sharma employed exponential function form to compute the growth rates for pre and post green revolution periods separately. They concluded that the production of pulses recorded negative growth rate in pre-green revolution period. They further concluded that the productivity of pulses was 1.21 per cent and 1.58 per cent during pre and post green revolution period respectively[49].

The present study used semi-log and second order semi log function to find out the compound growth rates of area. Production and productivity of Black gram (pulses) using time series data from 1956-57 to 1989-90 and two of its sub-periods namely per-green revolution period (1956-57) and post-green revolution period (1965-67 to 1989-90)

**Research Gap**

Most of the studies under review are relating to paddy, and the commercial crops. But the studies on pulses are scanty this is the main reason to choose the topic related to pulses. Hence, the present study is an attempt to study the economics of the pulses cultivation with select crops namely Black gram and Green gram in Thoothukudi district. The researcher has undertaken to analyse cost, return, determinants of yield, yield gap, supply responsiveness and labour observation in the cultivation Black and Green grams in the study area.

## CONCEPTS

The concepts reviewed in this section relate to production, costs and returns, resource-use efficiency, marketing margin, marketing cost, marketing efficiency, price-spread and the like.

**Production**

According to Kohls and Damey, production can be defined as the creation of utility in the process of making useful goods and services.[50] Again production can be defined as the process wherein some goods and services called inputs are transferred into other goods and services called output.[51]

According to Hanson, production covered the activities of changing the form of goods at any stage from raw material to the finished product, changing the situation of goods, changing the position of goods in time and the provision of some kind of services such as retailing, banking, entertaining and the like.[52] Production in the economic sense related to working on raw materials or natural resources in such a fashion that caused them to change their form change their chemical or physical capacities, to store them until their desire for them has become more urgent. [53]

In the present study, production represents the output of pulses resulting from the application of different inputs.

**Production Function**

Production function analysis helps to identify the uneconomic use of resources by the farmers. Chand defined production function as an algebraic relationship expressing an output in terms of a number of determinants – inputs or factors of production.[54] According to Handerson and Quandt, the production function was defined only for non-negative values of the inputs and outputs. It was constructed on the assumption that the quantities of fixed inputs were at pre-determined level, which the entrepreneur was unable to alter during the short-time period.[55]

Klein defined production function as a mathematical expression of technical relationship between input and output, which would remain constant as long as technology remained invariant.[56] Samuelson defined production function as one which indicated the maximum amount of output that could be produced by each of the specified inputs or factors of production and it was defined for a given state of technical knowledge.[57]

In the present study, production function is defined as the technological relationship between the output of pulses and the inputs, namely, area under pulses, human and bullock labour, seeds, manures and fertilizers and plant protection chemicals and the like.

**Productivity**

Heady defines productivity as the quantity of output turned out in a farm.[58] Bhattacharjee defined the term productivity to denote the output per unit of input in farm business.[59] Kargoanker indicated productivity as the ratio of output to input.[60] According to Gowar, productivity measures the efficiency with which the inputs are transferred into output.[61]

In the present study productivity is used as the quantity of output turned out per acre in the study area.

**Cost**

The cost of production is classified into variable (operational) costs and fixed costs.

**Variable Cost (Operational Cost)**

Variable cost or the operational cost is the cost incurred by a farmer on factors of production such as seeds, human labour, fertilizers, pesticides, bullock labour, livestock feed, tractor fuel and the like.

According to Tandon and Dhondyal, the variable costs are the prime costs, related to the variable resources.[62]

Shyamsundar et.al., included the cost of seeds, farm yard manure, fertilizers, plant protection chemicals, covering material, cost of irrigation, human labour, bullock labour and interest on working capital in the variable cost.[63]

In the present study, the variable cost or operational cost includes the expenses incurred in cash and kind. It includes the value of human labour, bullock labour, cost of irrigation, seeds, farm yard manure, fertilizers, plant protection chemicals, covering material and interest on working capital.

Rajagopalan[64] has included the following components in his study on the cost of production of crops in Tamil Nadu during the year 1978:

Cost A consists of the value of human labour including family labour, values of bullock labour, machinery charges, seeds, insecticides, manures and fertilizers, cost of irrigation and interest on working capital.

Cost C includes Cost A plus rent (including actual rent paid by the tenant or rental value of owned land) interest on fixed capital, land revenue, cess, taxes, and depreciation on implements and machinery.

In the present study, the cost of cultivation of pulses is classified into Cost A (Operational Cost- Cost A) and Cost C (Cost A plus fixed cost) which is generally adopted in farm management studies in India.

Cost A includes the following items:

*(i)* Human labour,
*(ii)* Bullock labour,
*(iii)* Chemical fertilizers,
*(iv)* Pesticides,
*(v)* Seed bulbs,
*(vi)* Farm yard manures,
*(vii)* Irrigation,
*(viii)* Interest on working capital,
*(ix)* Storage, packaging and transportation.

**Cost C includes the following items**

Cost A plus rent (includes actual rent paid by the tenant of rental value of owned land) interest on fixed capital excluding land cost plus land revenue, cess and taxes, depreciation on implements and machinery.

**Fixed Costs**

Fixed cost is the cost incurred on rent, tax, depreciation of implements and machinery, interest, insurance premium and the like. Fixed cost represents the total expenses incurred even when no output is produced but production has been committed in. It is often called overhead cost and usually includes contractual commitments for rental, maintenance, depreciation, overheads, salaries and wages. It is a sunk cost because it is quite unaffected by any variation in the level of output, during the period of time in which it is sunk.[65]

Lavanya et.al., included the depreciation of implements, machinery, buildings, interest on capital invested on owned land and rent on leased land under fixed cost.[66]

GREEN GRAM CULTIVATION

GREEN GRAM

BLACK GRAM CULTIVATION

BLACK GRAM

Kahlon and Sandhu included the depreciation on the value of capital assets and the interest on the value of capital investment under fixed cost. An additional item of rent paid or payable was also taken into account while working out the fixed cost.[67] Shyamsundar et.al., included the depreciation, interest on investment, land revenue and rental value of land in the fixed cost, for the production of rice.[68]

In the present study, fixed cost includes the rental value of land, land revenue, depreciation and interest on capital.

**Returns**

The estimation of returns from farm enterprises in its proper perspective is essential as it helps in assessing the efficiency of farm business as a whole and also the efficiency of resource-use in farms.

Kaul and Mehta defined gross income as the value of cash, the value of produce actually sold and the value of produce remaining in stock, all valued at harvest prices prevailing in that village.[69]

Tandon and Dhondyal defined net income as the gross income minus total expenses of production, namely, cost of seeds, manures, irrigation charges, wages of hired labourers and imputed value of unpaid family labour, depreciation, rent, interest on owned and working capital and marketing cost.[70]

Gupta explained net income as the income to the operator of land after deducting all items of expenditure such as paid out costs both in kind and cash, depreciation charges, land rent, interest on capital and imputed value for family labour from the total income of the farm.[71]

In the present study, gross returns are worked out by multiplying the value of produce by their respective market price. The net income is worked out from the gross returns minus the total cost (Cost C) which includes both fixed and operational costs.

## REFERENCES

1. B.D. Shukla, "Input-Output Relationship in Agriculture" *Indian Journal of Agricultural Economics,* Vol. 21, No. 3, 1966, p. 309.
2. V. Rajagopalan et.al. Studies on Cost of Production of Major Crops in Tamil Nadu, *Department of Agricultural Economics,* Tamil Nadu Agriculture University, Coimbatore, 1978, pp. 2-3.
3. V. Rajagopalan, et.al. *Studies on Cost of Production of Major Crops in Tamil Nadu,* Tamil Nadu Agricultural University, Coimbatore, 1978, p. 2-3.
4. Survey of Cost Production of Raw Cotton, *42nd Planary Meeting of the International Cotton Advisory Committee,* Memphis, USA Vol. 10, October 1983, p. 2.
5. David Groenfeldt, "Appreciating the Hidden Values of Paddy Cultivation Towards a New Policy Framework for Agriculture", *INWEPF/SY*/2004(03).
6. L.R. Kumar, K. Srinivas and S.R.K. Singh, "Technical Efficiency of Rice Farms under Irrigated Conditions of North West Himalayan Region — A Non-Parametric Approach", *Indian Journal of Agricultural Economics,* Vol. 60, No. 3, July-September, 2005, pp. 483-491.
7. A. Suresh and T.R. Keshava Reddy, "Resource-use Efficiency of Paddy Cultivation in Peechi Command Area of Thrissur District of Kerala: An Economic Analysis", *Agricultural Economics Research Review,* Vol. 19, January-June, 2006, pp 159-171.
8. A.A. Ansari and s. A. Ismail, "Paddy Cultivation In Sodic Soil Through Vermitech", *International Journal of Sustainable Crop Production,* Vol. 3(5) August 2008, pp. 123-139.
9. H. Basavaraja, S.B. Mahajanashetti and P. Sivanagaraju, "Technological Change in Paddy Production: A Comparative Analysis of Traditional and SRI Methods of Cultivation", *Indian Journal of Agricultural Economics,* Research Notes, Vol. 63, No. 4, October-December 2008, pp. 629-640.
10. M. Shivamurthy, L. Ramakrishna Rao, Shailaja Hittalamani and M. T. Lakshminarayan, "Constraints of Farmers Cultivating Rainfed Paddy in Eastern Dry Zone of Karnataka", *Mysore Journal of Agricultural Science,* Vol. 42(1), 2008, pp. 163-165.

11. Poduval, *loc.cit.*
12. V. Rajagopalan et.al., *Studies on Cost of Production in Tamil Nadu*, Department of Agricultural Economics, Tamil Nadu Agricultural University Coimbatore, 1978.
13. B.R. Davidson and B.R. Martin, "The Relationship between Yields on Farms and in Experiments", *Australian Journal of Agricultural Economics*, Vol. 9, No. 2, December 1965, pp. 129-1490.
14. K.K. Mokheyi, Gap Analysis-An Effective Production Increase Concept in Rice, *Summary of a Lecture Delivered at the State Leaven Training Meeting on Rice*, held at Purila Department of Agriculture West Bengal, India, July, 1977.
15. A. Tripathy, *A Study of Technological Gap in Adoption of New Rice Technology in Coolstal Orissa and Constraints Responsible for the Same*, (Unpublished Ph.D. Thesis, Indian Agricultural Research Institute, New Delhi, 1977).
16. K. Wanchai, A. Gomaz, "Basic Concepts, Objects and Approach Constraints to High Yields on Siren Rice Farms", *An Interim Report*, (Manila: International Rice Research Institute, 1977), p. 1.
17. D. David Rajarekan, *Yield Gap Analysis: A Study of Selected Crops in Madurai District (Paddy, Cholam, Cumbu, Groundnut)* (Unpublished M.Sc. (Agri) Thesis Submitted to Tamil Nadu Agricultural University, Coimbatore 1984), pp. 148-149.
18. S.D. Suryawanshi and N.S. Gaikward, "An Analysis of Yield Gap in Rabi Jowar in Drought Prone Area of Ahmednagar District", *Agricultural Situation in India*, Vol. 39, No. 3, 1984, pp. 147-153.
19. C.M. Chandrasekaran, Yield Gap Analysis in Sugarcane Crop in Awanashi Taluk, Coimbatore District (Unpublished M.Sc., (Agri) *Thesis Submitted to Department of Agricultural Economics*, Tamil Nadu agricultural University, Coimbatore, 1985), pp. 96-97.
20. J.B. Fale, G.G. Jahakare and S.G. Borude, "An Economic Analysis of Yield Gap in Rice in Retnagiri District", *Agricultural Situation in India*, Vol. 39, No. 2, 1985, pp. 925-930.
21. J.C. Flinn and Mubarak Ali, "Technical Efficiency in Basmati Rice Production", *Pakistan Journal of Applied Economics*, Vol. 5, No. 1, 1986, pp. 1-22.

22. P.N. Yadav and A.C. Gangwar, "Rice Production and Constraints in Bihar State", *Agricultural Situation in India,* Vol. 12, No. 1, 1986, pp. 9-13.

23. G. Subramaniyan and V. Nirmala, "Yield Gap Analysis in Rice Cultivation", *Southan Economist*, Vol. 27, No. 15, 1988, pp. 15-16.

24. R. Lakshmanan, *Constraints in Irrigated Groundnut: An Analytical Study of Yield and Technological Gap,* (Unpublished Ph.D., Thesis, Tamil Nadu Agricultural University, Coimbatore, 1986).

25. K. Kalirajan, "The Contribution of Location Specific Research to Agricultural Productivity", *Indian Journal of Agricultural Economics,* Vol. 35, No. 4, October-December, 1980, pp. 8-16.

26. L.J. Lau and P.A. Yolopoulos, "Profit Supply and Factor Demand Functions", *American Journal of Agricultural Economics,* Vol. 54, No. 1, February 1972, pp. 11-18.

27. R.K. Sampath, 'Nature and Measurement of Economic Efficiency in Indian Agriculture", *Indian Journal of Agricultural Economics,* Vol. 34, No. 2, April-June, 1979, p. 20.

28. L.J. Lau and P.A. Yolopoulos, "A Test for Relative Economic Efficiency and Application to Indian Agriculture", *American Economic Review,* Vol. 61, March, 1971, pp. 94-109.

29. M. Fure and D.L. McFadden, *Production Economics,* A Dual Approach to Theory and Application Noth-Holland Publishing Company Amsterdam, 1978, p. 13.

30. F.W. Shappand, *Cost and Production Function,* Princeton University Pren, Prinedon, 1953.

31. M. Fure and D.L. McFaden, *op.cit.,* p. 13.

32. A Zellner, "A Efficient Method for Estimating Seemingly Unrelated Regression and Test for Aggregation Bias", Vol. 57, No. 2, June 1962, pp. 348-375.

33. K. Kalirajan and J.C. Flinn, "Allorative Efficiency and Supply Response in Irrigated Rice Production", *Indian Journal of Agricultural Economics,* Vol. 36, No. 2, April-June, 1981, pp. 16-24.

34. P.N. Junankar, "Do Indian Farmers Maximise Profit?", *The Journal of Development Studies,* Vol. 17, No. 1, October 1980, pp. 48-61.

35. M.R. Abhi, P. Kumar and V.C. Mathur, "Technological Change and Factor Shares in Cotton Production: A Case Study of Akola Cotton Farms", *Indian Journal of Agricultural Economics*, Vol. XXXVIII, No. 3, July-September, 1983, pp. 407-15.
36. K. Kalirajan, "The Economic Efficiency of Farmers Growing High Yielding, Irrigated Rice in India", *American Journal of Agricultural Economics*, August, 1981, pp. 566-70.
37. R.K. Sampath, *Economic Efficiency in Indian Agriculture*, The Macmillan Company, Delhi, 1979, pp. 88-109.
38. K. Kalirajan and J.C. Flinn, *op.cit.*, pp. 16-24.
39. Pan A. Yolopoulos and L.J. Lau, "Resource use in Agriculture Application of the Profit Function to Selected Countries", *Food Research Institute Studies*, Vol. 17, No. 1, 1979, pp. 1-606.
40. P.A. Yolopoulos and L.J. Lau, "A Test for Relative Economic Efficiency: Some Further Results", *The American Economic Review*, Vol. LXIII, No. 1, March 1973, pp. 214-224.
41. Som. P. Pudasaini, *op.cit.*, pp. 48-55.
42. State Level Seminar on Increasing Productivity of Pulses in Tamilnadu National Pulse Research Centre 22-9-2000 by Mr. K. Seerangan.
43. Proceedings and Recommendations on Increasing Productivity of Pulses in Tamil Nadu-Seminar Proceedings on 22-9-2000 by Dr. S. Kanniyan.
44. Minutes-Paper Submitted by Gouroru on Tropical Soils in TNAV@ National Pulse Research Centre.
45. Subramanian K.V Growth of Horticulture Crops in India, Constrains and Opportunities Agriculture Situation in India 39 (5), 303, 1984.
46. Subramanian G and Vasanthi S.P "Agricultural Trends in Tamil Nadu 1961 to 1978 Agricultural Situation in India 43 (1); 25-27; 1988.
47. Survey of Indian Agriculture-2007.
48. Jawahar Thakur D.K. Singh and MiloRoy "An Analysis of Trends Growth and Technological Development Oilseed in Bihar.
49. Sharma S.K Sharma H.R and Sharma R.K Trends in Area Production and Yield of Commercial Crops in Indian Agricultural with Special Reference to Oil Seeds Agricultural Situation in India 44 (7); 581-585; 1989.

50. R.L. Kohls and W.D. Damey, *Marketing of Agricultural Product*, Mac Millan Company, New York, 1972, p. 72.
51. C.E. Bishop and W.D. Joussunit, *Agricultural Twin Analysis*, John Wiley and Sons, Inc., New York, 1958, p. 29.
52. J.C. Hanson, *A Text Book of Economics*, Leonard Hill, London,1972, pp. 21-22.
53. R.C. Curtis, *Economics for the Student*, Leonard Hill, London, 1963, p. 39.
54. Mahesh Chand, "On using Cobb-Douglas Production Function in Agriculture with Reference to India", *Indian Journal of Economics*, 48(189), 1967, p. 193.
55. J.M. Handerson and R.E. Quandt, *Micro-Economic Theory — A Mathematical Approach*, McGraw Hill Kogakusha Limited, Tokyo, 1971, p. 54.
56. Lawrence R. Klein, *An Introduction to Econometrics*, Prentice-Hall of India Private Limited, New Delhi, 1973, p. 84.
57. Paul A. Samuelson, *Economics*, McGraw Hill, Kogakusha Limited, Tokyo, 1973, p. 465.
58. Earl O. Heady, "Returns to Scale and Farm Size, Economics of Agricultural Productivity and Resource-use", *Journal of Farm Economics*, 34(2), 1952, pp. 348-351.
59. J.P. Bhattacharjee, "Resource-use and Productivity in World Agriculture", Journal of Farm Economics, 37(1), 1955, pp. 57-61.
60. M.C. Kargoanker, "Productivity: A Systems Approach", *Productivity*, 18(1), 1977, pp. 13-21.
61. Allan Gowar, "Productivity in Canadian Agriculture", *Canadian Journal of Agricultural Economics*, 28(2), 1980, pp. 95-96.
62. R.K. Tandon and S.P. Dhondyal, *Principles and Methods of Farm Management*, Nirbal-Kebal-Ram Press, Kanpur, 1978, p. 58.
63. M.S. Shyamsundar, *op.cit.*, p. 40.
64. V. Rajagopalan, *Studies on Cost of Production of Major Crops in Tamil Nadu*, Department of Agricultural Economics, Tamil Nadu Agricultural University, Coimbatore, 1978, pp. 2-3.
65. Paul A. Samuelson, *op.cit.*, p. 465.
66. S.J. Lavanya, M.M. Bala Rao and A.A. Pandu Ranga Rao, "Farm Finance by Banks — A Sample Study", *Eastern Economist*, 15(2), 1976, p. 43.

67. S.S. Kahlon and H.S. Sandhu, "Economic Evaluation of Dry Farming in Punjab", *Indian Journal of Agricultural Economics*, 26(4), 1971, pp. 334-342.
68. M.S. Shyamsundar, C. Nanja Reddy and N. Nagaraj, *op.cit.*, p. 40.
69. J.L. Kaul and S.K. Mehta, "Movement of Relative Shares of Factors of Production in Total Agricultural Income — A Study of Punjab Farmers", *Indian Journal of Economics*, 53(208), 1972, p. 14.
70. R.K. Tandon and S.P. Dhondyal, *op.cit.*, 1971, p. 341.
71. Ramesh Gupta, "Income Raising Potential on Rainfed Farm in Jabalpur District, Madhya Pradesh", *Indian Journal of Agricultural Economics*, 26(4), 1971, p. 354.

# CHAPTER 3

# Methodology and Profile of the Study Area

This chapter attempts to discuss the methodology adopted for the study. Further it describes the profile of the study area.

## METHODOLOGY

Designing a suitable methodology and selection of analytical tools are important for a meaningful analysis of any research problem. In this section an attempt is made to prepare a methodology of the present study. It includes sample design, collection of data, period of the study and tools of analysis.

### Sample Design

Multistage stratified random sampling technique has been adopted for the study, taking Thoothukudi district as the universe, the block as the stratum, the village as the primary unit and pulse cultivators as the ultimate unit.

Thoothukudi district comprises 12 blocks. Pulses are mainly cultivated in Kovilpatti, Vilathikulam and oottapidaram which show more than 70 per cent of area under pulses in this district and hence the selection of sample villages was restricted to these three blocks. A list of area under pulses in 2008-09 for all the villages of the three blocks was prepared from the records of the Joint Director of Agriculture, Thoothukudi. Five villages in each block, which account for the highest area under pulses cultivation in the descending order of magnitude, were selected as the study unit for primary data collection.

A list of pulses cultivators in the selected villages was obtained from the records of the Joint Director of Agriculture, Thoothukudi. The proportionate random sampling technique has been adopted to select 150 each of black gram and green gram farmers from these 15 villages.

## Collection of Data

### *Primary Data*

A reconnaissance survey of the study area was undertaken to form a crystal clear picture of the process and activities involved in pulse cultivation under actual farming conditions. Based on the information gathered a farm level, a detailed schedule was drafted, pre-tested and used in the field-survey. The objectives of the study were clearly explained to the farmers personally and their co-operation ensured. The details regarding the general characteristics of the sample farmers, farm structure, size of holding, cropping pattern, cost and returns, methods of sale, quantity retained, quantity sold and other aspects relating to the overall objectives of the study were collected from the sample farmers through the direct personal interview method. Even though the farmers did not maintain adequate farm records and accounts, they were able to furnish the particulars on the strength of their long association with farming. However to minimize recall bias, suitable cross checks and re-checks were carried out.

### *Secondary Data*

Secondary data were collected from:

*(i)* Directorate of Economics and Statistics, Government of Tamil Nadu, Chennai.

(ii) Office of Assistant Director of Economics and Statistics, Thoothukudi District.

In addition to that, books, journals and magazines were referred. Journals such as Indian Journal of Agricultural Marketing, Indian Journal of Agricultural Economics, Agricultural Marketing, Indian Journal of Marketing and other relevant journals were referred for collecting secondary data for the study.

**Period of the Study**

The field survey was conducted from September 2009 to March 2010 for the collection of primary data. This period relates to the main season for pulse cultivation in Thoothukudi district. The reference period of the survey is 2009-10.

**Method of Analysis**

Out of 300 sample farmer's cultivations pulses, 150 sample farms are under the category of black gram and remaining 150 sample farms come under green gram. In each crop, the sample farm can be divided into two group's namely small and large farmer based on area under pulses. For that, frequency tables were formed in each crop on the basis of area and its cumulative total was also worked out. The farms of less than 5 acres were grouped on small size and farms of more than or equal to 5 acres are grouped as large size. In the black gram, out of 150 sample farmers, 52 (34.67%) belong to small size and remaining 98 (65.33%) belong to large size. In the green gram, out of 150 sample farmers, 47 belong to small size and remaining 103 belong to large size.

**Tools of Analysis**

In order to analyse and compare cost and return structure of pulses, Cost A and Cost C concepts used by farm management studies have been adopted for the present study.

In order to identify and to compare the factors influencing yield of pulses for both groups of farmers, the following farm of multiple linear regression model was used.

$$\text{Log } Y = \propto_0 + \beta_1 \log X_1 + \beta_2 \log X_2 + \beta_3 \log X_3 + \beta_4 \log X_4 + \beta_5 \log X_5 + u$$

Where

Y = per acre yield in kgs.

$X_1$ = human labour per acre (in Rs.)

$X_2$ = bullock labour per acre (in Rs.)

$X_3$ = fertilizer per acre (in Rs.)

$X_4$ = pesticides per acre (in Rs.)

$X_5$ = capital flows in Rs. and

u = disturbance term.

$\propto_0, \beta_1, ........ \beta_5$ are the parameters to be estimated. The above model was estimated by the method of least squares.

The structural differences between two groups of farmers in each crop were examined by testing the equality of parameters of the above model by using Chow's test of the following formula.

$$F = \frac{\Sigma e^2 - (\Sigma e_1^2 + \Sigma e_2^2)k}{(\Sigma e_1^2 + \Sigma e_2^2)/n_1 + n_2 - 2k}$$

If the differences exist, the intercept and slope dummies were introduced in the model, to find out whether the differences occur at the intercept level or slope level or both. The model becomes

$$\log y = \propto_0 + \propto_1 D + \sum_{i=1}^{5} (\beta_i + r_i D) \log x_i + u$$

In the model, D is dummy variable representing 0 and 1, for small and large farmers respectively for each variety. The above model was estimated by using the method of least squares.

In order to compute demand and supply elasticities and to study absorption of labour, the normalised profit function was jointly estimated along with the four variable input demand functions with random disturbances of the following form.

$$\log \pi^* = \propto_0 + \beta_1^* \log W + \beta_2^* \log F + \beta_3^* \log P + \beta_4^* \log B + \propto_1^* \log c + u \;....$$

$$\frac{-W X_1}{\pi^*} = \beta_1 U_1$$

$$\frac{-F X_2}{\pi^*} = \beta_2 U_2$$

$$\frac{-P X_3}{\pi^*} = \beta_3 U_3$$

$$\frac{-B X_4}{\pi^*} = \beta_4 U_4$$

$\pi^*$ = Real Profit in Rupees (i.e. the total revenue minus total variable cost normalised by the price of output)

W = Real Wages for Labour

F = Real Fertilizer Price

P = Real Pesticides Price

B = Real Bullock pair day Price

A = Total area cultivated

C = Capital Flow (Calculated as the sum of depreciation, maintenance and opportunity cost of capital stock)

$X_1$ = Total labour man days utilised

$X_2$ = Total quantity of fertilizer used

$X_3$ = Total quantity of pesticides used

$X_4$ = Total bullock pair days and

u = Random disturbance.

The above models were estimated jointly by Zellner's Seemingly Unrelated Regression method.

Garrets ranking technique was adopted in order to rank the constraints of yield gap by the farmers cultivating pulses.

## PROFILE OF THE STUDY AREA

The usefulness of any research study can be fully appreciated only when the results are studied against the background information such as physical, social and economic conditions of the region. The present study was undertaken with the aim of highlighting the different aspects of pulses cultivation in Thoothukudi district.

### District at a Glance

The district started functioning as the twentieth District in Tamil Nadu with effect from October 20, 1986 with Thoothukudi as its headquarters. This district is located between 8°-05′ and 9°-30′ of northern latitude and 77°-05′ and 78°-25′ of the eastern longitude.

This district is bound by Virudhunagar and Ramanathapuram districts in the north, Kanyakumari district in the south, the Gulf of Mannar in the east and Tirunelveli district in the west. It is spread over an area of 4621 sq.kms.

### Administrative Regions

The district now consists of eight taluks namely Thoothukudi, Tiruchendur, Santhankulam, Srivaikuntam, Kovilpatti, Ottapidaram, Ettayapuram and Vilathikulam. It comprises two revenue divisions, seven revenue taluks and 12 development blocks. The administrative set up of the district is as follows:

The district has 20 town panchayats, 2 municipalities and 465 revenue villages. The district is industrially advanced with the majority of the industries located in and around Thoothukudi.

### Population Characteristics

The total population of the study area according to the 2001 census, was 15,65,743 of which 7,64,087 were males and 8,01,656 females. More than 50 per cent of the population was non workers. Of the total workers, 4.55 per cent were cultivators, 10.69 per cent were agricultural labours and 22.10 per cent were employed in other services including the household industry. The population and number of workers in Thoothukudi district are presented in table 3.1. The population density in the district is 315 per sq.kms . against the state average of 428 per sq.kms. The percentage of the urban population is 42.28 per cent and that of rural population is 57.72 per cent of the total population. The literacy percentage of male is 70.7 per cent and female is 56 per cent. Total literacy per cent of this district is 71.5 per cent.

**Table 3.1: Population and Number of Workers is Thoothukudi District (2009-10)**

| Sl.No. | Category | Number | Percentage |
|---|---|---|---|
| 1. | Population | 1565743 | |
| | Male | 764087 | 48.80 |
| | Female | 801656 | 51.20 |
| | Total | 15655743 | 100.00 |
| 2. | Cultivators | 71315 | 4.55 |
| 3. | Agricultural Labourers | 167387 | 10.69 |
| 4. | Marginal Workers | 88944 | 5.68 |
| 5. | Other Workers | 346036 | 22.10 |
| 6. | Non-Workers | 892061 | 56.98 |
| | **Total Population** | **1565743** | **100.00** |

*Source:* Assistant Director of Statistics, Thoothukudi.

## Climate and Rainfall

The district in general has a tropical climate except in the coastal areas. The mean maximum temperature ranges from 29.5°C to 40.5°C and the mean minimum temperature varies from 18.4°C to 26.7°C. May and August are the hottest months and the lowest temperature is recorded during December and January.

The district receives maximum rainfall from North-East and South-West monsoons. The season-wise annual average rainfall of Thoothukudi district is furnished in Table 3.2

**Table 3.2: Annual Average Rainfall of Thoothukudi District**

**(in mm.)**

| Year | South-West Monsoon (June-September) | North-East Monsoon (October-December) | Winter Period (January-February) | Hot Weather (March-May) | Total |
|---|---|---|---|---|---|
| 2006-07 | 78.58 | 270.36 | 31.80 | 67.31 | 448.05 |
| 2007-08 | 17.50 | 692.20 | 2.40 | 64.30 | 776.40 |
| 2008-09 | 107.30 | 519.91 | 7.20 | 74.80 | 709.21 |
| 2009-10 | 49.20 | 305.29 | 54.20 | 12.50 | 421.19 |

*Source:* Assistant Director of Statistics, Thoothukudi District.

## Rivers

The main river source for the district is the Tambiraparani River. The river flows through Srivaikuntam and Tiruchendur taluks and is the principal irrigation source of the district.

## Soils and Minerals

The soils found in Thoothukudi are of three types namely Black loam, Red sandy and alluvial soils. Black loamy soil is found in Kovilpatti, Vilathikulam, and Ottapidaram taluks. Sathankulam and parts of Tiruchendur and Thoothukudi taluks have red sandy soils. Alluvial soil is found in Srivaikuntam and parts of Tiruchendur taluks. The soils such as acidic, alkaline and saluro soils are found in the district. The acidic soil is found (1.15 per cent) in Thoothukudi, Srivaikuntam and Alwarthirunagari blocks.

This district is rich in mineral resources. Coral limestone is found in the east coast from Thoothukudi to Pamban. Lime shell and coral jelly are found in Thoothukudi taluk. Common salt is produced in the innumerable salt pans spread over nearly 17 Km. of coastal stretch from Veppoladai to Palayakayal. The salt produced here meets 30 per cent of the country's needs.

In the coastal range from Thoothukudi to Pamban, high grade coral limestone is found. Shell limestone is found near Arasur in Tiruchendur taluk.

## Transport and Communication

The district has a road length of 2310 km. comprising 1232 kms. of metallic road, 665 of non-metallic road and 413 kms. of kutcha road.

The district is served by 413 post officers covering 3270 persons per post office. There are 61 telegraphic offices in the district, which serve an average population of 22,140 per office. Similarly there is one radio set for every 31 person in the district.

## Port

Thoothukudi was a famous port city even in the olden days. Valuable commodities like pearls, chunks and salt were exported to various European countries from the ancient Port of Korkai. The activity of the Port increased enormously when large merchant vessels were able to berth in the Port.

## Industries

Southern Petro-Chemical Industries Company (SPIC) was established in 1975 with a capital outlay of Rs. 99 crores. The Heavy Water Plant (HWP) utilising free hydrogen from the SPIC plant is of natural importance, as heavy water is used as a moderator in atomic plants. Dhranga Dhara Chemical works is the other major industry of the district.

Also a number of small scale industries like match industry and textile industry are found in this district. Kovilpatti taluk is one of the major match manufacturing taluks in the state with more than 2000 small scale units located within the taluk.

## Fisheries

Thoothukudi is a major fishing centre. It is also considered to be the only pearl fishing centre in the whole of India. Fishing, next to agriculture, is an important occupation of the district. Nearly 35,000 MT of marine fish are produced per annum.

## Forestry

The area under forestry is 12724 hectares which occupies 2.77 per cent of the geographical area.

## Land-Use Pattern

Agro-climatic conditions of any region namely soil, irrigation, rainfall and the like, besides the ownership pattern of land, determine their use. The Thoothdukudi district extends over a geographical area of 4,59,054 hectares, of which net sown area accounts for 41.02 per cent. The pattern of land utilisation reveals that 2.40 per cent of the total geographical area is under forest and 4.28 per cent is barren and uncultivable land. Land put to non-agricultural uses is 15.63 per cent and cultivable waste is 4.31 per cent. Current fallows and other fallows form 13.33 per cent and 10.12 per cent of geographical area respectively. The pattern of land utilisation in Thoothukudi district is given in Table 3.3.

**Table 3.3: Land Use Pattern in the Thoothukudi District 2009-10**

| Sl. No. | Classification | Areas (in Hectares) | Percentage |
|---|---|---|---|
| 1. | Forests | 11012 | 2.40 |
| 2. | Barren Uncultivable lands | 19662 | 4.28 |
| 3. | Land put to non-agricultural uses | 71772 | 15.63 |
| 4. | Cultivable waste | 19779 | 4.31 |
| 5. | Permanent pastures and other grazing lands | 5132 | 1.12 |
| 6. | Land under miscellaneous tree crops | 35771 | 7.79 |
| 7. | Current fallows | 61189 | 13.33 |
| 8. | Other fallows | 46441 | 10.12 |
| 9. | Net area sown | 188296 | 41.02 |
| 10. | Total geographical area | 459054 | 100.00 |

*Source:* Assistant Director of Statistics, Thoothukudi District, 2009-10.

## Operational Holdings

The average size of land holdings of the district is 1.54 hectares as compared to 1.08 hectares in the state. Sixty-four per cent of the holdings are below 1 hectare and holdings with less than 2 hectares account for 83.50 per cent of the total number of holdings. Nearly 12 per cent of the holdings are between two and five hectares. Holdings with more than five hectares constitute 3.79 per cent of the total number. The distribution of land holdings in Thoothukudi district in 2009-10 is shown in Table 3.4.

**Table 3.4: Size-wise Distribution of Agricultural Holdings in Thoothukudi District (2009-10)**

| Size of Holdings (in Ha.) | Number of Operational Holdings | Percentage to Total Number of Holdings | Area Under the Holdings (in Ha.) | Percentage to Total Area |
|---|---|---|---|---|
| 0-0.5 | 92118 | 41.11 | 22889.83 | 8.06 |
| 0.5-1.0 | 53040 | 23.67 | 37642.50 | 13.26 |
| 1.0-2.0 | 41956 | 18.72 | 59406.95 | 20.92 |
| 2.0-3.0 | 16101 | 7.18 | 39358.40 | 13.86 |
| 3.0-4.0 | 7940 | 3.54 | 27493.61 | 9.68 |
| 4.0-5.0 | 4460 | 1.99 | 19902.81 | 7.01 |
| 5.0-7.5 | 4595 | 2.05 | 27836.45 | 9.81 |
| 7.5-10.0 | 2035 | 0.91 | 17229.31 | 6.07 |
| 10.0-20.0 | 1524 | 0.68 | 20173.95 | 7.11 |
| 20.0 and above | 333 | 0.15 | 11982.95 | 4.22 |
| **Total** | **224102** | **100.00** | **283916.76** | **100.00** |

*Source:* Assistant Director of Statistics, Thoothukudi District, 2009-10.

On the whole the majority of the holdings in the district are medium and small size holdings. The average size of holdings range from 0.91 hectares in Srivaikuntam taluk to 2.03 hectares in Vilathikulam taluk. The percentage of holdings ranging from 0.1 to 2.0 hectares to total holdings in each taluk is 72 per cent, 76 per cent, 72 per cent, 92 per cent, 88 per cent and 86 per cent in Kovilpatti, Ottapidaram, Vilathikulam, Sattankulam, Srivaikuntam, Tiruchendur and Thoothukudi taluks respectively.

## Irrigation

The main sources of irrigation in the district is through canals, tanks and wells accounting for 3,873 hectares, 18,040 hectares and 20,527 hectares of net area irrigated respectively during 2009-10. The gross area irrigated by canals has decreased from 12.09 per cent in 2009-10. The gross area irrigated by canals has decreased from 12.09 per cent in 1998-99 to 10.70 per cent in 2009-10. The gross area irrigated by tanks also has decreased from 44.10 per cent in 1998-99 to 44.17 per cent in 2009-10. The gross irrigated by well has increased from 38.82 per cent in 1998-99 to 45.12 per cent in 2009-10. The areas irrigated by different sources are presented in Table 3.5.

**Table 3.5: Area Irrigated by Different Sources in Thoothukudi District**

| Year | Net Area Irrigated | | | Total Gross Irrigated Area | | |
|---|---|---|---|---|---|---|
| | Canals | Tanks | Wells | Canals | Tanks | Wells |
| 1998-99 | 4873 (9.98) | 22145 (45.34) | 21825 (44.68) | 7218 (12.09) | 29323 (44.10) | 23183 (38.82) |
| 1999-2000 | 4346 (14.00) | 16471 (53.07) | 10219 (32.93) | 6708 (13.60) | 21611 (43.82) | 21001 (42.58) |
| 2007-08 | 3834 (9.35) | 15899 (38.74) | 21290 (51.90) | 4785 (11.12) | 16524 (38.41) | 21717 (50.47) |
| 2008-09 | 3945 (0.74) | 19687 (43.61) | 21508 (47.65) | 4468 (9.52) | 20505 (43.91) | 21722 (46.52) |
| 2009-10 | 3873 (8.13) | 18040 (42.51) | 20527 (48.37) | 5354 (10.70) | 22095 (44.17) | 22570 (45.12) |

*Source:* Assistant Director of Statistics, Thoothukudi District, 2009-10.

*Note:* Figures in brackets represent the percentage to total irrigated area.

Srivaikuntam and Tiruchendur taluks have the benefit of canal irrigation besides tank and well irrigation systems. Irrigation by tanks is widely prevalent in Thoothukudi and Tiruchendur taluks. Sattankulam and Kovilpatti taluks are irrigated mainly by wells.

The total net area of the district irrigated was 48,843 hectares in 1998-99 and the gross area irrigated was 59,724 hectares in 1998-99. In this period the net area sown and gross area sown accounted for 2,08,053 hectares and 2,22,471 hectares respectively. But in 2009-10, the net area irrigated and gross area irrigated decreased from 21.95 per cent and 26.85 per cent in 1998-99 to 21.54 per cent and 25.38 per cent in 2009-10 respectively. The net area sown is increased from 93.52 per cent in 1998-99 to 95.38 per cent in 2009-10.

The area irrigated by different sources in Thoothukudi district is furnished in Table 3.6.

**Table 3.6: Net and Gross Area Irrigated and Shown in Thoothukudi District**

**(in Hectares)**

| Year | Net Area Irrigated | Gross Area Irrigated | Net Area Shown | Gross Area Shown |
|---|---|---|---|---|
| 1998-99 | 48843 (21.95) | 59724 (26.85) | 208053 (93.52) | 222471 (100) |
| 1999-2000 | 41039 (21.59) | 49323 (25.95) | 178718 (94.02) | 190094 (100) |
| 2006-07 | 41026 (22.18) | 43029 (23.27) | 181699 (98.25) | 184932 (100) |
| 2007-08 | 45145 (23.78) | 46700 (24.60) | 187898 (98.98) | 189840 (100) |
| 2008-09 | 42516 (21.54) | 50101 (25.38) | 188296 (95.38) | 197413 (100) |

*Source:* Assistant Director of Statistics, Thoothukudi District, 2009-10.

*Note:* Figures in brackets represent percentage to total.

Area irrigated under major crops in Thoothukudi district is shown by Table 3.7.

**Table 3.7: Area Irrigated Under Major Crops in Thoothukudi District**

(in Hectares)

| Year | Pulses | Banana | Groundnut | Coconut | Cotton | Chillies | Betel Leaves |
|---|---|---|---|---|---|---|---|
| 1998-99 | 30120 (13.54) | 9989 (4.49) | 1100 (0.49) | 3817 (1.72) | 3100 (1.39) | 4273 (1.92) | 168 (0.09) |
| 1999-2000 | 22635 (11.91) | 9468 (4.98) | 639 (0.34) | 4137 (3.18) | 2205 (1.16) | 4511 (2.37) | 171 (0.09) |
| 2007-08 | 14409 (7.79) | 9256 (5.01) | 564 (0.31) | 4339 (2.35) | 1574 (0.85) | 4916 (2.66) | 163 (0.09) |
| 2008-09 | 17907 (9.43) | 9507 (5.01) | 656 (0.35) | 4510 (2.38) | 2217 (1.17) | 4566 (2.41) | 172 (0.09) |
| 2009-10 | 21659 (10.97) | 4972 (2.52) | 1285 (0.65) | 4694 (2.38) | 2039 (1.02) | 3780 (1.91) | 180 (0.09) |

*Source:* Assistant Director of Statistics, Thoothukudi District, 2009-10.

*Note:* Figures in brackets represent the percentage to gross irrigated area.

Table 3.7 reveals that area irrigated under pulses was 30120 hectares in 1998-99, but it has decreased from 13.54 per cent in 1998-99 to 10.97 per cent in 2009-10. The area irrigated under banana was 9989 hectares in 1998-99, 9468 hectares in 1999-2000 and 9256 hectares in 2007-08. In 2009-10 4972 hectares (2.53 per cent) irrigated were under banana cultivation.

## Cropping Pattern

The area under principal crops in Thoothukudi district is shown in Table 3.8.

**Table 3.8: Area Under Principal Crops in Thoothukudi District**

**(in Hectares)**

| Year | Pulses | Banana | Groundnut | Coconut | Cotton | Chilly |
|---|---|---|---|---|---|---|
| 2005-06 | 30120 (13.53) | 9989 (4.49) | 4059 (1.82) | 2723 (1.22) | 30670 (13.79) | 16414 (9.38) |
| 2006-07 | 22635 (11.91) | 9468 (4.98) | 4321 (2.27) | 2039 (1.07) | 24832 (13.06) | 18602 (9.78) |
| 2007-08 | 14409 (7.71) | 9256 (5.01) | 4567 (2.47) | 1527 (0.83) | 18978 (10.26) | 20347 (11.00) |
| 2008-09 | 17907 (9.43) | 9507 (5.01) | 4627 (2.44) | 1727 (0.91) | 17660 (9.30) | 20394 (10.74) |
| 2009-10 | 21721 (11.01) | 9472 (4.80) | 4764 (2.41) | 2762 (1.40) | 17450 (8.84) | 24342 (12.33) |

*Source:* Assistant Director of Statistics, Thoothukudi District, 2009-10.

*Note:* Figures in brackets represent the percentage to gross sown area.

The most predominantly cultivated crop with an area of 30670 hectares was cotton, followed by pulses (30,120 hectares), Chilly (16,414 hectares) and banana (9,989 hectares), in 2005-06. During the year 2009-10, cultivated crop with an area of 24,342 hectares was chilly followed by pulses, cotton and banana with 21,721 hectares, 17,450 hectares and 9,472 hectares respectively. The area under pulses has declined from 13.53 per cent in 2005-06 to 11.01 per cent in 2009-10. The area under banana has increased from 4.49 per cent in 2005-06 to 4.80 per cent in 2009-10.

# CHAPTER 4

# Analysis of Cost and Return Structure

An attempt had been made in this chapter to study the characteristics of sample farmers, labour utilisation, input and output structure, cost and returns for Large and Small farmers cultivating Black Gram and Green Gram of pulses. For the purpose of analysis, Black Gram is expressed as BG and Green Gram is expressed as GG. For comprehensive analysis, this chapter has been divided into three sections namely:

*(i)* Characteristics of sample farmers

*(ii)* Labour utilisation and input output structure

*(iii)* Cost and returns structure

## CHARACTERISTICS OF SAMPLE FARMERS

This section attempts to discuss the characteristics regarding age, education, family size, members engaged in cultivation, size of operational holdings and experience of the selected sample farmers.

### Age-wise Distribution

The distribution of age of the sample farmers is presented in Table 4.1.

**Table 4.1: Age-wise Distribution of Sample Farmers**

| Age (in years) | Black Gram (BG) | | | Green Gram (GG) | | |
|---|---|---|---|---|---|---|
| | Large | Small | Overall | Large | Small | Overall |
| Less than 30 | 9 (6.00) | 5 (3.33) | 14 (9.33) | 5 (3.33) | 3 (2.00) | 8 (5.33) |
| 30-40 | 60 (40.00) | 24 (16.00) | 84 (56.00) | 60 (40.00) | 25 (16.67) | 85 (56.67) |
| 40-50 | 22 (14.67) | 12 (8.00) | 34 (22.67) | 24 (16.00) | 12 (8.00) | 36 (24.00) |
| Above 50 | 7 (4.66) | 11 (7.34) | 18 (12.0) | 14 (9.33) | 7 (4.67) | 21 (14.0) |
| **Total** | **98 (65.33)** | **52 (34.67)** | **150 (100)** | **103 (68.66)** | **47 (31.33)** | **150 (100)** |

*Source:* Survey Data.
Figures in brackets represent percentages to total.

Table 4.1 shows that in Black Gram, 78.67 per cent of the farmers were in the age group of 30 to 50 years. The age group of 40-50 years was relatively lower in the case of Small farmers (8.00%) while it was 14.67 per cent in the case of Large farmers to their respective totals. The farmers below 30 years constitute only 9.33 per cent to the total. There above 50 years form 12.00 per cent only.

In case of Green Gram, the farmers below 30 years constitute only 5.33 per cent to the total. Those above 50 years form 14.00 per cent only. The respondents between the age group 30 to 50 years constitute 80.67 per cent. The age group of 30-40 years was relatively higher in the case of Large farmer (40.00%) while it was only 16.67 per cent in the case of Small farmers.

Comparing these two crops, it is found that the farmers between age group of 30 to 50 years were found high in Green Gram (80.67%) while it was 78.67 per cent in the case of Black Gram.

## Literacy Levels

The distribution of literacy level of sample farmers is shown in Table 4.2.

**Table 4.2: Literacy Levels of Sample Farmers**

| Literacy Level | Black Gram (BG) | | | Green Gram (GG) | | |
|---|---|---|---|---|---|---|
| | Large | Small | Overall | Large | Small | Overall |
| Illiterate | 3 (2.00) | 3 (2.00) | 6 (4.00) | 2 (1.33) | 3 (2.00) | 5 (3.34) |
| School level | 78 (52.00) | 36 (24.00) | 114 (76.00) | 82 (54.67) | 23 (15.33) | 105 (70.00) |
| College level | 14 (9.33) | 12 (8.00) | 26 (17.33) | 14 (9.33) | 18 (12.0) | 32 (21.33) |
| Professional and others | 3 (2.00) | 1 (0.67) | 4 (2.67) | 5 (3.33) | 3 (2.00) | 8 (5.33) |
| **Total** | **98 (65.33)** | **52 (34.67)** | **150 (100)** | **103 (68.66)** | **47 (31.35)** | **150 (100)** |

*Source:* Survey data.
Figures in bracket represent percentages to total.

Table 4.2 reveals that in Black Gram 76.00 per cent of the farmers in the study area had only school education, followed by those with college level education (17.33%). The illiterates form 4.00 per cent to the total. The school level education percentage was higher among Large farmers (52.00%) than among Small farmers (24.00%), while in the case of college level education, the Large farmers (9.33%) was considered to be higher than the Small farmers (8.00%).

In Green Gram, farmers having the college level education form 21.33 per cent to the total. It was found that 70.00 per cent of the farmers are the study area had only school education, followed by illiterates (3.34%). The school level education percentage was higher among Large farmers (54.67%) than among Small farmers (15.33%) respectively.

Black Gram was found to be high in school level educated farmer (76.00%) when compared with Green Gram (70.00%). And illiterates are low in Green Gram (3.34%) when compared with Black Gram.

## Distribution of Family Size

The distribution of family size of sample farmers is presented in Table 4.3.

**Table 4.3: Family Size of the Sample Farmers**

| Size (in Nos.) | Black Gram (BG) | | | Green Gram (GG) | | |
|---|---|---|---|---|---|---|
| | Large | Small | Overall | Large | Small | Overall |
| Less than 4 | 29 (19.33) | 13 (8.67) | 42 (28.00) | 24 (16.00) | 12 (8.00) | 36 (24.00) |
| 4-6 | 60 (40.00) | 34 (22.67) | 94 (62.67) | 70 (46.67) | 31 (20.67) | 101 (67.33) |
| 6-8 | 7 (4.67) | 3 (2.00) | 10 (6.66) | 9 (6.00) | 3 (2.00) | 12 (8.00) |
| 8 and above | 2 (1.33) | 2 (1.33) | 4 (2.67) | – | 1 (0.66) | 1 (0.67) |
| **Total** | **98 (65.33)** | **52 (34.67)** | **150 (100)** | **103 (68.67)** | **47 (31.33)** | **150 (100)** |

*Source:* Survey data.

Figures in bracket represent percentages to total.

From Table 4.3 in the Black Gram it is clear that nearly 70.00 per cent of the farmers had a family size of more than four members while only 2.67 per cent of the farmers had a family size of more than 8. The major dominant family size in the case of Small farmers group was 4-6 which constituted 22.67 per cent to the total. In case of large farmers it was 4-6 members which constituted 40.00 per cent to the total.

In Green Gram the major dominant family size in the case of Small farmers group was 4-6 which constituted 20.67 per cent to the total. In case of Large farmers it was 4-6 members which constituted 46.67 per cent to the total. It is clear that nearly 24.00 per cent of the farmers had a family size less than 4. While only 0.67 per cent of the farmers had a family size of more than 8.

When comparing these two crops, it is found low in the Black Gram of the farmers had a family size of 4-6 is 62.67 per cent but in case of Green Gram, the farmers it was 4-6 members which constituted 67.33 per cent to the total. The use of family labour was more in case of Black Gram when compared to the Green Gram.

## Family Members Engaged in Cultivation

The distribution of number of family members engaged in cultivation is given in Table 4.4.

**Table 4.4: Number of Family Members Engaged in Farming Activity**

| Number of Members | Black Gram (BG) | | | Green Gram (GG) | | |
|---|---|---|---|---|---|---|
| | Large | Small | Overall | Large | Small | Overall |
| Below 2 | 21 (14.00) | 12 (8.00) | 33 (22.00) | 25 (16.67) | 12 (8.00) | 37 (24.67) |
| 2-4 | 56 (37.33) | 35 (23.34) | 91 (60.67) | 62 (41.33) | 21 (14.00) | 83 (55.33) |
| 4-6 | 15 (10.00) | 3 (2.00) | 18 (12.0) | 11 (7.33) | 10 (6.67) | 21 (14.00) |
| Above 6 | 6 (4.00) | 2 (1.33) | 8 (5.33) | 5 (3.33) | 4 (2.66) | 9 (6.00) |
| **Total** | **98 (65.33)** | **52 (34.67)** | **150 (100)** | **103 (68.67)** | **47 (31.33)** | **150 (100)** |

*Source:* Survey Data.
Figures in bracket represent percentages to total.

Table 4.4 shows that in Black Gram 22.00 per cent of the sample farmers had utilised 1 to 2 members of their family in pulse cultivation, of which 14.00 per cent were Large farmers and 8.00 per cent were Small farmers respectively. But 60.67 per cent utilised 2-4 members in cultivation of which 37.33 per cent were Large farmers and 23.34 per cent were Small farmers.

In the case of Green Gram 55.33 per cent of the sample farmers had utilised 2-4 members of their family in pulse cultivation. Which constitutes 41.33 per cent of the Large farmers and 14.00 per cent of Small farmers. And 24.67 per cent utilised 1-2 members in cultivation of which 16.67 per cent were Large farmers and 8.00 per cent were Small farmers.

Black Gram was found to be a higher usage of family labour than the Green Gram. In Black Gram 22.00 per cent of farmers had utilised 1 to 2 members, but it was high in Green Gram, 24.67 per cent of sample farms had been utilised.

## Distribution of Size of Operational Holdings

Table 4.5 depicts the distribution of size of operational holding of sample farmers.

**Table 4.5: Size of Operational Holdings of the Sample Farmers**

| Size of Holdings (in acres) | Black Gram (BG) | | | Green Gram (GG) | | |
|---|---|---|---|---|---|---|
| | Large | Small | Overall | Large | Small | Overall |
| Less than 1 | 15 (10.00) | – | 15 (10.00) | 13 (8.67) | – | 13 (8.67) |
| 1-2 | 25 (16.67) | – | 25 (16.67) | 22 (14.67) | – | 22 (14.67) |
| 2-5 | 58 (38.66) | – | 58 (38.67) | 68 (45.33) | – | 68 (45.33) |
| 5-8 | – | 42 (28.00) | 42 (28.00) | – | 41 (27.33) | 41 (27.33) |
| Above 8 | – | 10 (6.67) | 10 (6.66) | – | 6 (4.00) | 6 (4.00) |
| **Total** | **98 (65.33)** | **52 (34.67)** | **150 (100)** | **103 (68.67)** | **47 (31.33)** | **150 (100)** |

*Source:* Survey data.
Figures in bracket represent percentages to total.

Table 4.5 reveals that in Black Gram, nearly 65.34 per cent of the operational holding was below 5 acres and remaining 34.66 per cent were above 5 acres. Among Large farmers, the dominant operational holding was between 2-5 acres (38.67%) while in the Small farm, it was 5-8 acres (28.00%) to the total.

In the case of Green Gram, nearly 68.67 per cent of the operational holding was below 5 acres. The remaining 31.33 per cent belong were above 5 acres. Among Large farmers, the dominant operational holding was between 2-5 acres (45.33%) while in the Small farms, it was 5-8 acres (27.33%) to the total.

Comparing these two crops, Black Gram is low in operational holdings below 5 acres (65.34%) while Green Gram is high in operational holding below 5 acres (68.67%) respectively.

**Farming Experience of Sample Farmers**

The distribution of farming experience of sample farmers is given in Table 4.6.

**Table 4.6: Experience of Sample Farmers in Pulses Cultivation**

| Experience in Years | Black Gram (BG ) | | | Green Gram (GG) | | |
|---|---|---|---|---|---|---|
| | Large | Small | Overall | Large | Small | Overall |
| Less than 5 | 10 (6.67) | 4 (2.67) | 14 (9.33) | 4 (2.67) | 5 (3.33) | 9 (6.00) |
| 5-10 | 26 (17.33) | 10 (6.67) | 36 (24.00) | 27 (18.00) | 15 (10.00) | 42 (28.00) |
| 10-15 | 57 (38.00) | 36 (24.00) | 93 (62.00) | 64 (42.67) | 23 (15.33) | 87 (58.00) |
| 15-20 | 5 (3.33) | 2 (1.33) | 7 (4.67) | 8 (5.33) | 4 (2.67) | 12 (8.00) |
| **Total** | **98 (65.33)** | **52 (34.67)** | **150 (100)** | **103 (68.67)** | **47 (31.33)** | **150 (100)** |

*Source:* Survey Data.
Figures in bracket represent percentages to total.

It is observed from Table 4.6 that in Black Gram 24.00 and 62.00 per cent of the farmers have had the experience of 5-10 years and 10-15 years respectively. While 9.33 per cent of farmers had the experience of less than 5 years and only 4.67 per cent of farmers have experience of 15-20 years.

In Green Gram 28.00 and 58.00 per cent of the farmers had experience of 5-10 years and 10-15 years. While 8.00 per cent of the farmers had experience between 15-20 years and only 6.00 per cent had experienced less than 5 years.

Comparatively, Green Gram has 58.00 per cent of farmers with experience of 10-15 years, whereas in Black Gram 62.00 per cent of farmers had experienced between 10 to 15 years.

## LABOUR UTILISATION AND INPUT OUTPUT STRUCTURE

An attempt is made in this section to analyse the labour utilisation and input-output structure for Black Gram (BG) and Green Gram (GG) of Pulses in the study area.

### Labour Utilisation

Labour is one of the major constituents of the total cost incurred in farm business and therefore it has a direct impact on farm earnings. Labour utilisation is influenced by the size of the farm, cropping pattern and the intensity of cropping. Availability of labour decides the crop combinations to be selected as some are labour intensive and others are less so. In order to understand the labour absorption in BG of pulses, labour utilisation for both BG and GG of pulses is presented in Table 4.7.

**Table 4.7: Labour Utilisation in the Cultivation of BG and GG Variety of Pulses**

(Rs./Acre)

| Sl. No. | Particulars | Black Gram (BG) | | | Green Gram (GG) | | |
|---|---|---|---|---|---|---|---|
| | | Large Farmers | Small Farmers | Overall Farmers | Large Farmers | Small Farmers | Overall Farmers |
| 1. | Human labour | 996.25 (78.99) | 1001.68 (79.49) | 998.13 (79.16) | 1141.07 (83.48) | 1060.37 (82.55) | 1115.75 (83.20) |
| 2. | Bullock labour | 264.99 (21.01) | 258.40 (20.51) | 262.71 (20.84) | 225.84 (16.52) | 224.18 (17.45) | 225.32 (16.80) |
| 3. | Total labour cost | 1261.24 (100) | 1260.08 (100) | 1260.84 (100) | 1366.91 (100) | 1284.55 (100) | 1341.07 (100) |

*Source:* Survey data.
Figures in brackets represent percentages to total.

Table 4.7 reveals that there was a direct proportion between the size of the farm and the human labour and total labour cost in the case of Black Gram. The total labour cost increased with the increase in size of the farm. The total labour cost per acre was Rs. 1261.24 for Large farmers and Rs. 1260.08 for Small farmers. In the total labour cost, the cost of human labour constituted 78.99 per cent for Large farmer, 79.49 per cent for Small farmers and 79.16 per cent for overall farmers. Bullock labour constituted for 21.01 per cent on Large farmers, 20.51 per cent on Small farmers and 20.84 per cent on overall farmers.

In the case of Green Gram, the total labour cost per acre was from Rs. 1366.91 for Large farmers and Rs. 1284.55 for Small farmers. In the total labour cost, the cost of human labour constituted 83.48 per cent, 82.55 per cent and 83.20 per cent for Large, Small and overall farmers respectively. Bullock labour accounted for 16.52 per cent for Large farmers, 17.45 per cent for Small farmers and 16.80 per cent for overall farmers.

The classification of human labour utilisation in BG and GG of pulses cultivation is reported in Table 4.8.

**Table 4.8: Classification of Human Labour Utilisation in the Cultivation of BG and GG of Pulses**

(Rs./Acre)

| Sl. No. | Particulars | Black Gram (BG ) | | Green Gram (GG) | |
|---|---|---|---|---|---|
| | | Large Farmers | Small Farmers | Large Farmers | Small Farmers |
| 1. | Family Labour | 187.46 (18.81) | 350.29 (34.97) | 201.74 (17.68) | 354.27 (33.41) |
| 2. | Permanent Labour | 87.27 (8.76) | – | 89.23 (7.82) | – |
| 3. | Casual Labour | 721.58 (72.43) | 651.39 (65.03) | 850.10 (74.50) | 706.61 (66.59) |
| 4. | Total hired labour (2+3) | 808.85 (72.43) | 651.39 (65.03) | 939.33 (82.32) | 706.61 (66.59) |
| 5. | Total Labour cost (1+4) | 996.25 (100) | 1001.68 (100) | 1141.07 (100) | 1060.37 (100) |

*Source:* Survey data.

It is seen from Table 4.8 that for BG of pulses, the contribution of hired human labour was low (65.03%) on Small farmer group and higher (72.43%) on Large farmer group. Permanent labourers were employed in large farmer group 8.76 per cent and they were absent in the case of small farmer.

Family labourers on Large and Small farms accounted 18.81 per cent and 34.97 per cent respectively. The total labour cost worked out to Rs. 996.25 and Rs. 1001.68 per acre on Large and Small farmers respectively.

Whereas in the case of Green Gram of pulses, the contribution of hired human labour was higher (82.32%) on large farmer group and lower (66.59%) on small farmer group. Family labourers on Large and Small farms constituted 17.68 per cent and 33.41 per cent respectively. The total labour cost was worked out to Rs. 1141.07 for Large farmers and Rs. 1060.37 for Small farmers.

**Input-Output Structure**

The input-output structure of pulses cultivation for Large and Small farmers under BG and GG is shown in Table 4.9.

In order to test the difference between mean input-output structure of farmers cultivating BG and GG of pulses, the following form of Z-test was carried out.

$$\text{Z-test} = \frac{\text{Difference}}{\text{SE difference}}$$

Since the computed Z-value is greater than table value of Z at 5 per cent level (1.96) the difference is significant, otherwise it is not significant.

**Table 4.9: Input-Output Structure Per Acre for Large and Small Farmers Cultivating BG and GG of Pulses**

| Sl. No. | Particulars | Black Gram (BG) | | | Green Gram (GG) | | |
|---|---|---|---|---|---|---|---|
| | | Large Farmers | Small Farmers | Z-test | Large Farmers | Small Farmers | Z-test |
| 1 | 2 | 3 | 4 | 5 | 6 | 7 | 8 |
| 1. | Human Labour (in mandays) | 8.30 | 8.47 | 1.65 | 9.37 | 9.01 | 1.13 |
| 2. | Bullock labour (in pairs) | 2.21 | 2.19 | 1.09 | 2.18 | 2.88 | 1.54 |

*(Contd...)*

| 1 | 2 | 3 | 4 | 5 | 6 | 7 | 8 |
|---|---|---|---|---|---|---|---|
| 3. | Fertilizers (in Rs.) | 331.30 | 315.21 | 3.24* | 395.88 | 356.27 | 3.31* |
| 4. | Pesticides (in Rs.) | 162.12 | 152.03 | 5.15* | 206.36 | 196.87 | 4.21* |
| 5. | Seeds (in Rs.) | 141.24 | 146.84 | 1.06 | 126.65 | 132.09 | 1.01 |
| 6. | Yield (in kg) | 181.61 | 194.12 | 3.99* | 182.31 | 196.12 | 5.43* |
| 7. | Sample size | 98.00 | 52.00 | | 103.00 | 47.00 | |

*Source:* Survey data.

* Indicates significance at 5 per cent level.

It is revealed from Table 4.9 that the yield per acre of BG of pulses was 181.61 kgs for Large farmers and 194.12 kgs for Small farmers. This shows that there is a significant difference in the yield between Large and Small farmers. The difference in yield works out to 12.51 kgs. In the case of human labour, the amount of labour required was 8.30 man days for the Large farmers and 8.47 man days for Small farmers. The Large farmers applied 331.30 kgs of fertilizer whereas the Small farmers used 315.21 kgs of fertilizer. In the case of pesticides, Large farmers used 162.12 kgs and Small farmers used 152.03 kgs respectively.

Apart from yield, the differences in the utilisation of other input variables like, fertilisers and pesticides were also found to be significant between the Large and Small farmers in the study area. With regard to the use of other variables like human labour, bullock labour and seeds, the differences between Large and Small farmers were not found to be significant.

Whereas in the case of Green Gram of pulses, the yield per acre was 182.31 kgs for Large farmers and 196.12 kgs for Small farmers. It is observed that difference in the yield is significant between Large and Small farmers cultivating Green Gram also. The difference in yield works out 13.81 kgs. The human labour required was 9.37 man days and 9.01 man days for Large and Small farmers respectively. The Large farmers used 395.88 kgs of fertilizer whereas the Small farmers applied 356.27 kgs of fertilizer. In the case of pesticides, 206.36 kgs and 196.87 kgs were used by Large and Small farmer respectively.

Apart from yield, the differences in the utilisation of other input variables like fertilizers and pesticides were also found to be significant between Large and Small farmers in the study area. The differences in the utilisation of variables namely, human labour, bullock labour and seeds between Large and Small farmers were not found to be significant.

Thus, it may be concluded from the above analysis that as in the case of BG of pulses, the small farmers were efficient in the use of inputs like fertilizers and pesticides and small farmers have produced more yields per acre than Small farmers.

## COST AND RETURNS STRUCTURE

In this section, the cost and returns structures of Large and Small farmers producing pulses are studied in order to understand the differences in BG and GG farm management. For this purpose, the collected data have been analysed with reference to cost and returns structure including various cost components used in the study area.

### Cost Components

In agricultural operations, the cost of cultivation refers to the expenses incurred on the various inputs to obtain the final produce. In the present study, cost has been categorised into cost A (operational cost) and cost C (cost A plus fixed cost and rent a land). Cost of production of pulses is calculated based on the following assumption.

The cost of human labour was calculated at the price of Rs. 300 per man-day which is the prevailing wage rate during the period under study. In the case of woman labour, 2 woman-days of eight hours each were considered as one man-day unit on the basis of prevailing wage rate (Rs. 100 per man-day). The existing wage rate was considered alike and valued by hired labour and family labour. Similarly, the actual expenses incurred by the farmers were considered for both hired and owned bullock pairs. The cost of bullock labour per pair per day was Rs. 250 which included the cost of human labour engaged along with the bullock pairs.

The actual amounts paid by the farmers towards the cost of fertilizers, pesticides and farm manures were considered. In the case of owned manure, market value at the rate of Rs. 180 per cart load was uniformly taken. The actual expenses incurred on seeds per acre during the study period were considered and these included both transportation and seed treatment changes. Regarding the land rent, the existing rental value of the owned land in the study area was taken into account. Annual interest on farm assets was estimated at 11 per cent on the basis of the interest rate charged by the Land Development Bank for a long -term loan. The farm assets were evaluated on the basis of the values given by the farmers during the interview.

The Co-operative Banks charged the annual interest on loan which was calculated at 12 per cent based on the rate of interest for short-term loans. The cost items included the actual payment made for land revenue. The expenses incurred on irrigation were included.

**Cost and Returns Structure of Black Gram (BG)**

Per acre average cost and returns structure of Large and Small farmers cultivating BG of pulses, are furnished in Table 4.10. (*See Table on next page*)

It is understood from Table 4.10 that the Large farmers produced 181.61 kgs of pulses and earned Rs. 7371.53 per acre while their net returns per acre were Rs. 4,760.81. In the case of Small farmers, the yield per acre was 194.12 kgs and they realised Rs. 7764.80 per acre as gross returns while their net return per acre was Rs. 5170.48. In overall yield per acre, gross returns and net returns earned were 185.95 kgs, Rs. 7507.86 and Rs. 4902.83 per acre respectively. It indicates that the small farmers were getting higher yield and thereby higher net income than large farmers in the case of BG.

**Table 4.10: The Per Acre Average Cost and Returns Structure of Large and Small Farmers Cultivating Black Gram**

| Sl. No. | Cost Component | Large Farmers | Small Farmers | Overall Farmers |
|---|---|---|---|---|
| 1. | Human labour (including family labour) | 996.25 | 1001.68 | 998.13 |
| 2. | Bullock labour | 264.99 | 258.40 | 262.71 |
| 3. | Chemical fertilizer | 331.30 | 315.21 | 325.72 |
| 4. | Pesticide cost | 162.12 | 152.03 | 158.62 |
| 5. | Seed cost | 141.24 | 146.84 | 143.18 |
| 6. | Farm manure | 182.49 | 179.79 | 181.55 |
| 7. | Cost of Mechanical Power | 77.80 | 103.52 | 86.72 |
| 8. | Interest on working capital | 182.23 | 155.48 | 172.96 |
| | Cost A | 2338.42 | 2312.87 | 2329.59 |
| 9. | Rent | 163.17 | 171.49 | 166.05 |
| 10. | Interest as fixed capital (excluding land cost) land revenue, less and taxes, depreciation of implements and machinery | 109.13 | 110.00 | 109.41 |
| | Total – Cost C (total) | 2610.72 | 2594.36 | 2605.05 |
| | Yield per acre in kg | 181.61 | 194.12 | 185.95 |
| | Gross Returns (Rs.) | 7371.53 | 7764.80 | 7507.86 |
| | Net Returns (Rs.) | 4760.81 | 5170.48 | 4902.83 |

*Source:* Survey data.

The cost analysis reveals that per acre total cost, that is operational cost of cultivation for Large farmers, worked out to Rs. 2338.42, whereas it was Rs. 2312.87 for Small farmers. It in observed that total cost incurred was found lower in the case of Small farmer compared to Large farmers.

The cost of human labour forms the major component of the total cost of production for both Large and Small farmers. Next to human labour, the amount spent on the use of chemical fertilizers occupied the major portion in the total cost of production. It came behind the cost of farm manure, cost of irrigation, pesticides, seed cost and bullock labour. The costs of all the inputs except bullock labour were found to be higher for Small farmer than for Large farmers. Thus, it is inferred from the analysis that the small farmers were found more efficient than the large farmers, both cost-wise and return wise.

The percentage of various cost components to total cost (Cost C) is presumed in Table 4.11.

**Table 4.11: Per Acre Percentage Cost of Various Cost Components to Total Cost of Black Gram**

| Sl. No. | Cost Component | Large Farmers | Small Farmers | Overall Farmers |
|---|---|---|---|---|
| 1. | Human labour (including family labour) | 38.16 | 38.61 | 38.32 |
| 2. | Bullock labour | 10.15 | 9.96 | 10.09 |
| 3. | Chemical fertilizer | 12.69 | 12.15 | 12.50 |
| 4. | Pesticide cost | 6.21 | 5.86 | 6.09 |
| 5. | Seed cost | 5.41 | 5.66 | 5.50 |
| 6. | Farm manure | 6.99 | 6.93 | 6.97 |
| 7. | Cost of Mechanical Power | 2.98 | 3.99 | 3.33 |
| 8. | Interest on working capital | 6.98 | 5.99 | 6.64 |
| | Cost A | 89.57 | 89.15 | 89.43 |
| 9. | Rent | 6.25 | 6.61 | 6.37 |
| 10. | Interest as fixed capital (excluding land cost) land revenue, less and taxes, depreciation of implements and machinery | 4.18 | 4.24 | 4.20 |
| | Cost C (Total) | 100.00 | 100.00 | 100.00 |

*Source:* Survey data.

Table 4.11 reveals that the percentage cost a variable inputs (Cost A) to total cost (Cost C) was 89.57 per cent for Large farmers, 89.15 per cent for Small farmers and 89.43 for overall farmers. In Cost A, human labour cost was found to be high for Large, Small and overall farmers at 38.16 per cent, 38.61 per cent and 38.32 per cent respectively followed by cost of chemical fertilizers. The Large farmers spent 12.69 per cent of their total cost on the utilisation of chemical fertilizer while Small farms and overall farms spent 12.15 per cent and 12.50 per cent respectively. Next to this the major cost component was cost of bullock labour which constituted 10.15 per cent, 9.96 per cent and 10.09 per cent of the total cost for Large, Small and overall farmers respectively. Cost of pesticides worked out to 6.09 per cent for the Large farmer, while it was 5.86 per cent and 6.21 per cent for Small farmers and all farmers respectively. Farm manure constituted 6.99 per cent, 6.93 per cent and 6.97 per cent for Large, Small and overall farmers respectively. The rent for land was higher for Small farmers than in the case of Large farmer. It accounted for 6.25 per cent and 6.61 per cent for Large farmers and Small farmers.

Interest as farm assets, depreciation of implements and machinery involved 4.18 per cent of the total cost for Large farmer and 4.24 per cent of the total cost for Small farmers.

The percentage of various cost components to total cost (Cost C) is shown as angular pie diagram on Large and Small farmers in Figure 4.1. (*See fig. on next page*)

**Economics of Cultivating Black Gram (BG)**

The details of the economics of cultivating Black Gram (BG) of pulses in the case of Large and Small farmers are furnished in Table 4.12. (*See Table on page 90*)

It is observed from Table 4.12 that the economics of cultivating pulses for Large and Small farmers cultivating Black Gram of pulses the input-output ratios in terms of operational cost and total cost were found to be Rs. 3.15 and Rs. 2.82 respectively for Large farmers and Rs. 3.36 and Rs. 2.98 respectively for Small farmers. The cost benefit ratio for Large farmers showed that each rupee spent on pulses cultivates resulted in a benefit of Rs. 1.82 per acre and in case of Small farmers it was Rs. 1.98.

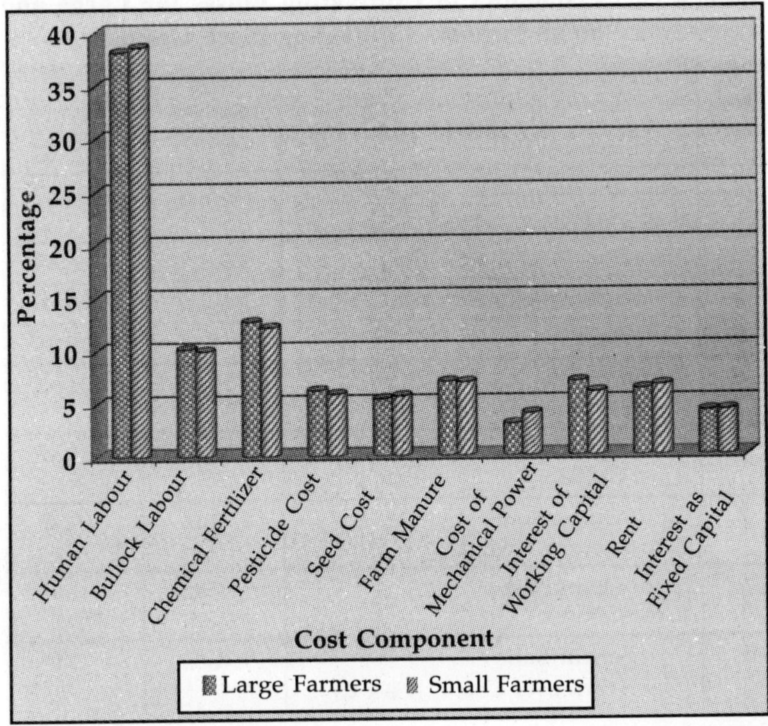


*Fig. 4.1:* **Pre Acre Percentage Cost of Various Cost Components to Total Cost of Black Gram**

The economics of cultivating pulses revealed that the cultivation by small farmers was more beneficial in terms of both yield and profit per acre. The total cost was higher for the large farmer, indicating the requirement of a more intensive care in use of inputs.

## Cost and Returns Structure of Green Gram (GG)

Table 4.13 (*See Table on page 90*) furnishes information on the average cost and returns structure of Large and Small farmers cultivating GG of pulses.

**Table 4.12: Economics of Cultivating Pulses for Large and Small Farmers Cultivating Black Gram**

| Sl. No. | Particulars | Large Farmers | Small Farmers |
|---|---|---|---|
| 1. | Gross return (Rs.) | 7371.53 | 7764.80 |
| 2. | Total operating cost (Cost A) (Rs.) | 2338.42 | 2312.87 |
| 3. | Net return over Cost A (Rs.) | 5033.11 | 6,563.45 |
| 4. | Total production cost (Cost C) (Rs.) | 2610.72 | 2594.36 |
| 5. | Net return over cost (Cost C) (Rs.) | 4760.81 | 5170.48 |
| 6. | Cost of production per kg. (Cost A) (Rs.) | 12.88 | 11.92 |
| 7. | Cost of production per kg. (Cost C) (Rs.) | 14.38 | 13.42 |
| 8. | Input-Output Ratio (Gross return/Cost A) | 3.15 | 3.36 |
| 9. | Input-Output Ratio (Gross return/Cost C) | 2.82 | 2.98 |
| 10. | Cost-Benefit Ratio (Net return over Cost C (Cost C) | 1.82 | 1.98 |

*Source:* Survey data.

**Table 4.13: The Per Acre Average Cost and Returns Structure of Large and Small Farmers Cultivating Green Gram**

| Sl. No. | Cost Component | Large Farmers | Small Farmers | Overall Farmers |
|---|---|---|---|---|
| 1 | 2 | 3 | 4 | 5 |
| 1. | Human labour (including family labour) | 1141.01 | 1060.37 | 1115.75 |
| 2. | Bullock labour | 225.84 | 224.18 | 225.32 |
| 3. | Chemical fertilizer | 395.88 | 356.27 | 383.47 |
| 4. | Pesticide cost | 206.36 | 196.87 | 203.38 |
| 5. | Seed cost | 126.65 | 132.09 | 128.35 |

*(Contd...)*

| 1 | 2 | 3 | 4 | 5 |
|---|---|---|---|---|
| 6. | Farm manure | 188.64 | 154.62 | 177.98 |
| 7. | Cost of Mechanical Power | 78.23 | 74.63 | 77.10 |
| 8. | Interest on working capital | 211.08 | 181.94 | 201.95 |
| | Cost A | 2573.69 | 2380.97 | 2513.30 |
| 9. | Rent | 265.40 | 271.78 | 267.41 |
| 10. | Interest as fixed capital (excluding land cost) land revenue, less and taxes, depreciation of implements and machinery | 113.06 | 163.63 | 128.92 |
| | Total – Cost C (total) | 2952.16 | 2816.38 | 2909.62 |
| | Yield per acre in kg | 182.31 | 196.12 | 186.64 |
| | Gross Returns (Rs.) | 9115.50 | 9806.28 | 9331.94 |
| | Net Returns (Rs.) | 6163.34 | 6989.90 | 6422.32 |

*Source:* Survey data.

It is inferred from Table 4.13 that in the case of farmers cultivating Green Gram of pulses, the Large farmers produced 182.31 kgs of green gram and earned Rs. 9115.50 while their net returns were Rs. 6163.34. In the case of Small farmers produced 196.12 kgs of green gram and earned Rs. 9806.28 whereas their net returns were Rs. 6989.90. In overall, yield per acre, gross returns and net return earned were 186.64 kgs, Rs. 9331.94 and Rs. 6422.32 per acre respectively. It indicates that the small farmers were getting higher yield and thereby higher net income than large farmers.

The cost analysis shows that per acre total cost, that is operational cost of cultivation for Large farmers, worked out to Rs. 2573.69 whereas it was Rs. 2380.97 for Small farmers. It is observed that total cost incurred was found higher in the case of large farmers compared to small farmers.

The cost of human labour forms the major component of the total cost of production for both Large and Small farmers. Next to human labour comes the amount spent on the use of chemical fertilizers. It came behind the cost of farm manure, cost of irrigation, pesticides, seed cost and bullock labour. The costs of all the inputs except bullock labour were found to be higher for Small farmer than for Large farmers. Thus, it is revealed from the analysis that as in BG of pulses, the small farmers were found more efficient than the large farmers, both cost-wise and return wise in the case of producing Green Gram also.

The per acre percentage of various cost components are given in Table 4.14.

**Table 4.14: Per Acre Percentage Cost of Various Cost Components to Total Cost of Green gram**

| Sl. No. | Cost Component | Large Farmers | Small Farmers | Overall Farmers |
|---|---|---|---|---|
| 1. | Human labour (including family labour) | 38.65 | 37.65 | 38.34 |
| 2. | Bullock labour | 7.65 | 7.96 | 7.75 |
| 3. | Chemical fertilizer | 13.41 | 12.65 | 13.68 |
| 4. | Pesticide cost | 6.99 | 6.99 | 6.99 |
| 5. | Seed cost | 4.29 | 4.69 | 4.41 |
| 6. | Farm manure | 6.39 | 5.49 | 6.12 |
| 7. | Cost of Mechanical power | 2.65 | 2.65 | 2.65 |
| 8. | Interest on working capital | 7.15 | 6.46 | 6.94 |
| | Cost A | 87.18 | 84.54 | 86.38 |
| 9. | Rent | 8.99 | 9.65 | 9.19 |
| 10. | Interest as fixed capital (excluding land cost) land revenue, less and taxes, depreciation of implements and machinery | 3.83 | 5.81 | 4.43 |
| | Cost C (Total) | 100.00 | 100.00 | 100.00 |

*Source:* Survey data.

Table 4.14 reveals that the percentage cost on variable inputs (Cost A) to total cost (Cost C) was 87.18 per cent for Large farmers, 84.54 per cent for Small farmers and 86.38 per cent for overall farmers. In Cost A, human labour cost was found to be high for Large, Small and overall farmers at 38.65 per cent, 37.65 per cent and 38.34 per cent respectively followed by cost on chemical fertilizers. The Large farmers spent 13.41 per cent of the total cost on utilisation of chemical fertilizers while Small farmers and overall farmers spent 12.65 per cent and 13.68 per cent respectively. Next to this, the major cost component was the cost of bullock labour which constituted 7.65 per cent, 7.96 per cent and 7.75 per cent of the total cost for Large, Small and overall farmer respectively. Cost of pesticides worked out to 6.99 per cent for Large farmers, 6.99 per cent for Small farmers and 6.99 per cent for overall farmers. Interest paid on working capital constituted 7.15 per cent, 6.46 per cent and 6.94 per cent for Large, Small and all farmers respectively. Interest on farm assets, depreciation of implements and machinery involved 3.83 per cent of the total cost for Large farmers and 5.81 per cent for Small farmers in the case of Green Gram of cultivating pulses.

Thus, it may be concluded that the expenditure on inputs exhibited almost similar pattern in both crops of pulses as well as farmer groups. Rajagopalan[1] et.al. And Harrison[2] reported similar results.

The percentage of various cost components to total cost (Cost C) is shown as angular pie diagram for Large and Small farmers in Figure 4.2 (*See Fig. on next page*).

Table 4.15 (*See Table on page 95*) presents comparative information on the economics of cultivating GG of pulses by the Large and Small farmer groups.

It is inferred from Table 4.15 that the input-output ratios in terms of operational cost and total cost were found to be Rs. 3.54 and Rs. 3.13 respectively for Large farmers and Rs. 4.11 and Rs. 3.148 per acre respectively for Small farmers in the case of Green Gram of pulses. The cost-benefit ratio for Large farmers showed that each rupee spent on pulses cultivation resulted in a benefit of Rs. 2.13 per acre and for Small farmers it was Rs. 2.48.

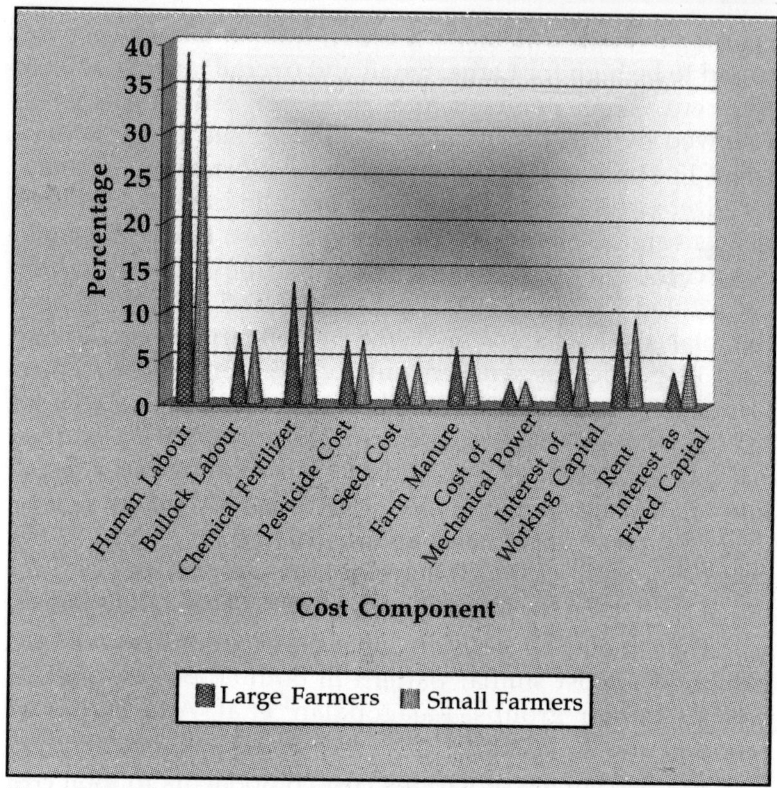


*Fig. 4.2:* **Per Acre Percentage Cost of Various Cost Components to Total Cost of Green Gram**

The economics of cultivating GG of pulses showed that the cultivation of small farmer was more beneficial in terms of both yield and profit per acre. The total cost was higher for the large farmers, indicating the requirement of a more intensive care in use of inputs in the study area.

**Table 4.15: Economics of Cultivating Pulses in Large and Small Farmers Cultivating Green gram**

| Sl. No. | Particulars | Large Farmers | Small Farmers |
|---|---|---|---|
| 1. | Gross return (Rs.) | 9115.50 | 9806.28 |
| 2. | Total operating cost (Cost A) (Rs.) | 2573.69 | 2380.97 |
| 3. | Net return over cost A (Rs.) | 6541.81 | 7425.31 |
| 4. | Total production cost (Cost C) (Rs.) | 2952.16 | 2816.38 |
| 5. | Net return over cost (Cost C) (Rs.) | 6203.34 | 6989.90 |
| 6. | Cost of production per kg. (Cost A) (Rs.) | 14.12 | 12.14 |
| 7. | Cost of production per kg. (Cost C) (Rs.) | 15.97 | 14.36 |
| 8. | Input-Output Ratio (Gross return/Cost A) | 3.54 | 4.11 |
| 9. | Input-Output Ratio (Gross return/Cost C) | 3.13 | 3.148 |
| 10. | Cost–Benefit Ratio (Net return over Cost C (Cost C) | 2.13 | 2.48 |

*Source:* Survey data.

## REFERENCES

1. V. Rajagopaln, *Studies on Cost of Production of Major Crops in Tamil Nadu*, Department of Agricultural Economics, Tamil Nadu Agricultural University, Coimbatore, 1978.
2. James Quigley Harrison, *Agricultural Modernisation and Income Distribution: An Economic Analysis of the Impact of New Seed Crops on the Crop Production of Small and Large Farms in India* (Mimeo) Ph.D., Princeton University, 1972.

# CHAPTER 5

# Determinants of Yield Yield Gap and Constraints

The main focus of this chapter is to identify and compare the variables, which identify the yield of pulses for Large and Small farmers cultivating Black Gram (BG) and Green Gram (GG) in the study area. It also examines the yield gap arising out of the difference between the maximum and the average yield at farm level under each group of farmers. It further investigates the yield constraints, which prevent the Large farmers from achieving the potential yield at farm level in the study area.

## THE ANALYTICAL FRAMEWORK

The determinants of yield per acre for Large and Small farmers producing pulses are identified with the help of multiple linear regression models of Cobb-Douglas type. Per acre yield is taken as the dependent variable and five factor inputs are included as independent variables. The regression model fitted was of the form.

$$Y = \propto_0 + \beta_1 \log X_1 + \beta_2 \log X_2 + \beta_3 \log X_3 + \beta_4 \log X_4 + \beta_5 \log X_5 + U \qquad (5.1)$$

where

$Y$ = Per acre yield in kgs

$X_1$ = Human labour per acre (in Rs.)

$X_2$ = Bullock labour per acre (in Rs.)
$X_3$ = Fertilizer per acre (in Rs.)
$X_4$ = Pesticides per acre (in Rs.)
$X_5$ = Capital flows per acre (in Rs.) and
U = Disturbance term

The structural difference between the two sample farmers, Small and large, was tested by using Chow's test.

$$F = \frac{\Sigma e^2 - (\Sigma e^2_1 + \Sigma e_2^2)/k}{(\Sigma e^2_1 + \Sigma e^2_2)/n_1 + n_2 - 2k} \qquad (5.2)$$

where,

k = The number of parameters including the intercept term.

$\Sigma e^2$ = Unexplained or residual sum of squares of the sample corresponding to both Large and Small farmers.

$\Sigma e^2_1$ = Unexplained or residual sum of squares of the sample corresponding to Large farmers.

$\Sigma e_2^2$ = Unexplained or residual sum of squares of the sample corresponding to small farmers.

$n_1$ = Sample size of Large farmers; and

$n_2$ = Sample size of Small farmers.

The 'F' test was carried out and if the computed value of 'F' was less than the table value of F at 5 per cent level of significance with ($k, n_1+n_2-2k$) degrees of freedom the null hypothesis that there was no structural difference between the two groups of farmers could be accepted. If there was a structural difference between the two groups, the test whether the difference occurs and at the interceptor at the slope level or at both had to be conducted by incorporating the dummy variables at the intercept and slope levels in the regression model.

The structural difference between the two groups of farmers was tested by using the regression model of the following form:

$$\log Y = \propto_0 + \propto_1 D + \sum_{i=1}^{5} \beta i \log X + \sum_{i=1}^{5} r_j \, D \log X_i + u \qquad (5.3)$$

In the model (5.3) D was the dummy variable. The dummy variable D stood 0 for the Large farmers and 1 for the Small farmers.

## ESTIMATED RESULTS OF REGRESSION MODEL FOR BLACK GRAM

The regression model (5.1) was estimated by the method of least squares for Large, Small and overall farmers cultivating Black Gram (BG) of pulses separately. The estimated results are presented in Table 5.1

**Table 5.1: Estimated Regression Results for Large and Small Farmers Cultivating Black Gram**

| Variable | Parameter Estimates | | |
|---|---|---|---|
| | Large Farmers | Small Farmers | Overall Farmers |
| Intercept | 3.6511 | 2.8911 | 2.8516 |
| Log $X_1$ | 0.3215* | 0.3141* | 0.3014* |
| | (3.9916) | (3.4541) | (2.9861) |
| Log $X_2$ | 0.0911 | 0.0671 | 0.0822 |
| | (0.0661) | (1.0173) | (1.0466) |
| Log $X_3$ | 0.3116* | 0.2915* | 0.2818* |
| | (3.7615) | (2.9861) | (3.1421) |
| Log $X_4$ | 0.1248* | 0.0919* | 0.1141* |
| | (2.8161) | (3.1981) | (3.1761) |
| Log $X_5$ | 0.3141* | 0.3341* | 0.3262* |
| | (2.7115) | (4.0121) | (3.9516) |
| $R^2$ | 0.7945 | 0.8161 | 0.7961 |
| F-Value | 28.4621 | 31.1621 | 31.4152 |
| Residual Sum of Squares | 0.092 | 0.088 | 0.265 |
| No. of Observations | 98 | 52 | 150 |

Figures in bracket represent t-value.

* Indicates that the co-efficients are statistically significant at 5 per cent level.

It is observed from Table 5.1, in the case of Large farmers, $R^2$ value indicated that about 79.45 per cent of variations in yield were jointly caused by the five explanatory variables included in the model. Human labour and fertilizer were found to be statistically significant at 5 per cent levels. It indicated that one per cent increase in these variables could increase yield by 0.3215 per cent, 0.3116 per cent, 0.1248 per cent and 0.3141 per cent respectively. It was also found that the human labour had a greater influence on the determination of yield, followed by the variable fertilizer. As per F-value, the fitted regression model was statistically significant at 5 per cent level.

As far as the Small farmers were concerned, all the five explanatory variables together accounted for nearly about 81.61 per cent variables in yield. All the five variables were positively related to yield. Human labour, fertilizer and capital flows emerged statistically significant at 5 per cent level, indicating the one per cent increase in these variables could increase yield per acre by 0.3141 per cent, 0.2915 per cent, 0.0919 per cent and 0.3341 per cent respectively. The impact of capital flow on yield of pulses was found to be higher in the case of Small farmers. The F-value showed that the estimated regression model was statistically significant at 5 per cent level.

In the case of overall farmers, the five independent variables jointly accounted for about 79.61 per cent of the variations in the yield of pulses. All the five variables had a positive effect on the determination of yield. Input variables such as human labour, fertilizers, pesticides and capital flow were found to be significantly related to the yield of pulses. It indicated that an additional percentage of use of these variables was capable of increasing the yield by 0.3014 per cent, 0.2818 per cent, 0.1141 per cent and 0.3262 per cent per acre respectively. Capital flows were found to be the most influential input on yield determination of pulses, followed by the variables human labour and fertilizer. The F-value showed that the overall regression model emerged statistically significant at 5 per cent level.

Thus it may be concluded from the analysis that the explanatory variables included in the model together explained about 79 to 81 per cent of the observed variability in the yield of pulses in the case of Large, Small and overall farmers. Human labour was found to be the most significant input influencing the yield of pulses in the case of Large farmers producing Black Gram. Whereas in the cases of Small farmers and overall farmers, capital flow had a greater influence on yield of pulses.

## TEST FOR STRUCTURAL DIFFERENCES

In order to examine the structural differences between Large and Small farmers producing Black Gram of pulses, Chow's test (5.2) was carried out. The results are given in Table 5.2.

**Table 5.2: Test for Equality of Parameters Between Large and Small Farmers Producing Black Gram**

| $\sum e^2$ | $\sum e_1^2$ | $\sum e_2^2$ | $(n_1+n_2-2k)$ | F | (6,138) at 1 per cent Level | Inference |
|---|---|---|---|---|---|---|
| 0.265 | 0.092 | 0.088 | 138 | 11.41 | 2.85 | Structural difference exists between Large and Small farmers |

From Table 5.2, the result of chow's test shows that the computed F-value (F) was higher than the table F-value and it was statistically significant at 1 per cent level. It indicates that structural difference existed between Large and Small farmers producing Black Gram.

## TESTS OF THE STABILITY OF INTERCEPT AND SCOPE

In order to identify the factors causing structural difference between two groups of farmers producing Black Gram, dummy variables were incorporated both at the slope and the intercept levels in the regression model (5.3). The model (5.3) was estimated by the method of least squares and the results are given in Table 5.3.

**Table 5.3: Tests for Stability of Intercept and Slope Between Large and Small Farmers Producing Black Gram**

| Variable | Parameter Estimate | t-value |
|---|---|---|
| Intercept | 2.9916 | |
| Intercept dummy – D | 0.0681 | 1.0148 |
| log $X_1$ | 0.3561* | 4.3216 |
| log $X_2$ | 0.1142 | 0.0763 |
| log $X_3$ | 0.3141* | 4.1921 |
| log $X_4$ | 0.0751 | 0.0991 |
| log $X_5$ | 0.3861* | 3.6561 |
| D log $X_1$ | -0.0421 | -0.0062 |
| D log $X_2$ | 0.0492 | 0.0549 |
| D log $X_3$ | -0.0261* | 3.7516 |
| D log $X_4$ | 0.0564 | 1.0126 |
| D log $X_5$ | 0.0419 | 0.0783 |
| $R^2$ | 0.8061 | |
| F-Value | 35.61 | |
| No. of Observations | 150 | |

* Indicates that the co-efficient are statistically significant at 5 per cent level.

It is found from Table 5.3 that in the case of Large farmers, all the explanatory variable had a positive impact on yield per acre. Out of the five, three variables namely human labour, fertilizers and capital flows emerged statistically significant at 5 per cent level. A percentage increase in these variables was capable of increasing yield by 0.3561, 0.3141 and 0.3861 per cent respectively. It is found that the human labour was the most influential variable in relation to yield, followed by fertilizer.

The Small farmers revealed that a structural difference was found due to the variable fertilizer. It indicates that an additional percentage of fertilizer was capable of increasing the yield of Large farmers by 0.3141 per cent and Small farmers by 0.288 [0.3141 + (-0.0261)] per cent. It is observed from the analysis that fertilizer had a greater effect on the yield of Large farmers than the Small farmers producing Black Gram. The F-value shows that the fitted regression model was statistically significant at one per cent level.

The dummy coefficient corresponding to the intercept is not statistically significant. It reveals that there is no difference between two groups of farmers with regard to technological change. It implies that the nature of technological change is neutral for both groups of farmers. It indicates that the yield curve of Large farmers had shifted neutrally in relation to that of Small farmers. In the slope dummy, the co-efficient corresponding to fertilizer emerged statistically significant. This implies that the structural difference between the two groups of farmers was caused with respect to the variable fertilizer.

## ESTIMATED RESULTS OF REGRESSION MODEL FOR GREEN GRAM

The regression model (5.1) was fitted by the method of least squares for Small, Large and overall farmers producing Green Gram (GG). The results are presented in Table 5.4.

**Table 5.4: Estimated Regression Results for Large and Small Farmers Cultivating Green Gram (GG)**

| Variable | Parameter Estimates | | |
|---|---|---|---|
| | Large Farmers | Small Farmers | Overall Farmers |
| 1 | 2 | 3 | 4 |
| Intercept | 2.1561 | 2.7661 | 2.1718 |
| Log $X_1$ | 0.3161*<br>(2.7716) | 0.3162*<br>(3.4161) | 0.2961*<br>(3.0461) |
| Log $X_2$ | 0.0431<br>(0.0613) | 0.1141<br>(0.0913) | 0.0791<br>(0.0769) |
| Log $X_3$ | 0.3218*<br>(4.1931) | 0.3145*<br>(3.7916) | 0.3019*<br>(2.7962) |
| Log $X_4$ | 0.0761<br>(0.1121) | 0.1015<br>(0.0049) | 0.0999<br>(0.0481) |

*(Contd...)*

| 1 | 2 | 3 | 4 |
|---|---|---|---|
| Log $X_5$ | 0.3162* (3.1260) | 0.3162* (2.9861) | 0.2945* (4.1142) |
| $R^2$ | 0.7861 | 0.8151 | 0.7919 |
| F- Value | 22.65 | 27.18 | 26.41 |
| Residual Sum of Squares | 0.036 | 0.039 | 0.219 |
| No. of Observations | 103 | 47 | 150 |

Figures in bracket represent t-value.

* Indicates that the co-efficient are statistically significant at 5 per cent level.

It is inferred from Table 5.4 that in the case of Large farmers, $R^2$ value indicated that about 78.61 per cent of variation in yield were jointly caused by the five explanatory variables included in the model. Human labour, fertilizer and capital flows were found to be statistically significant at 5 per cent level. It indicated that one per cent increase in these variables could yield by 0.3161 per cent, 0.3218 per cent and 0.3162 per cent per acre respectively. It was also found that the fertilizer had a greater influence on the determination of yield, followed by the variables, human labour and capital flows. As per F-value, the fitted regression model was statistically significant at 1 per cent level.

As far as the Small farmers were concerned, all the five explanatory variables together accounted for nearly 81.51 per cent variation in the yield. Out of five variables included in the regression model, human labour, fertilizers and capital flows were found to be statistically significant at 5 per cent level. It indicated that one per cent increase in these variables could increase yield per acre by 0.3162 per cent, 0.3145 per cent and 0.3162 per cent respectively. The impact of capital flows on yield of pulses was found to be higher in the case of Small farmers. The F-value showed that the estimated regression model was statistically significant at 1 per cent level.

In the case of total farmers, the five independent variables jointly accounted for about 79.19 per cent of the variations in the yield of pulses. All the five variables had a positive effect on the determination of yield. Input variables such as human labour, fertilizer and capital flow were found to be significantly related to the yield of Green Gram. It indicated that on additional percentage of use of these variables, it was capable of increasing the yield by 0.2961 per cent, 0.3019 per cent and 0.2945 per acre respectively. Fertilizer was found to be most influential input on yield determination of Green Gram, followed by the variables, capital flows and human labour. The F-value showed that the overall regression model emerged statistically significant at 1 per cent level.

Thus, it may be concluded from the analysis of Green Gram of pulses farmers, fertilizer was found to be a significant variable in the case of Large farmers. Whereas in the case of Small farmers, capital flows were the most important variable influencing the yield of pulses.

## TEST FOR STRUCTURAL DIFFERENCES

Table 5.5 highlights the results of Chow's test (5.2) used to examine whether any structural differences existed between Large and Small farmers producing Green Gram of pulses in the study area.

**Table 5.5: Test for Equality of Parameters Between Large and Small Farmers Producing Green Gram (GG)**

| $\sum e^2$ | $\sum e_1^2$ | $\sum e_2^2$ | $(n_1+n_2-2k)$ | F | (6,138) at 1 per cent Level | Inference |
|---|---|---|---|---|---|---|
| 0.216 | 0.038 | 0.040 | 138 | 43.65 | 2.82 | Structural difference exists between Large and Small farmers |

From the Table 5.5, the result of chow's test shows that the computed F-value (F*) was higher than the table F-value and it was statistically significant at 1 per cent level. It indicates that structural difference existed between Large and Small farmers producing of Green Gram.

## TESTS OF THE STABILITY OF INTERCEPT AND SLOPE

In order to find out the variables causing structural difference between Large and Small farmers producing Green Gram of pulses, slope and intercept dummy variables were incorporated in the regression model (5.1). The model (5.3) was estimated by the method of least squares and the results are shown in Table 5.6.

**Table 5.6: Test for Stability of Intercept and Slope Between Large and Small Farmers Producing Green Gram (GG)**

| Variable | Parameter Estimate | t-Value |
|---|---|---|
| Intercept | 3.1141 | |
| Intercept dummy – D | 1.0049 | 1.1241 |
| log $X_1$ | 0.2861* | 3.7541 |
| log $X_2$ | 0.0869 | 0.0481 |
| log $X_3$ | 0.3141* | 2.9962 |
| log $X_4$ | 0.1128 | 1.0961 |
| log $X_5$ | 0.3192* | 3.7545 |
| D log $X_1$ | 0.0185 | 1.1172 |
| D log $X_2$ | 0.0614 | 0.0083 |
| D log $X_3$ | 0.1145 | 0.0473 |
| D log $X_4$ | 0.0109 | 1.0122 |
| D log $X_5$ | 0.0174* | 3.1992 |
| $R^2$ | 0.7919 | |
| F-Value | 33.4611 | |
| No. of observations | 150 | |

* Indicates that the coefficients are statistically significant at 5 per cent level.

It is inferred from Table 5.6, in the case of Large farmers, all five explanatory variables had a positive impact on yield per acre. Out of five crops, three variables namely human labour, fertilizers and capital flows emerged statistically significant at 5 per cent level. A percentage increase in these variables was capable of increasing yield by 0.2861 per cent,

0.3141 per cent and 0.3192 per cent respectively. It is observed that the capital flows were the most influential variable in relation to yield, followed by the fertilizers.

In the case of Small farmers it is revealed that the structural difference was found due to the variable capital flows. It indicates that an additional percentage of capital flows was capable of increasing the yield of Large farmers by 0.3192 per cent and Small farmers by 0.3366 per cent (0.3192 + 0.0174). It is observed from the analysis that capital flows had a greater effect on the yield of Small farmers than that of Large farmers. The F-value shows that the fitted regression model was statistically significant at 1 per cent level.

As in the case of Black Gram, the dummy co-efficient corresponding to intercept is also not statistically significant for Green Gram. It reveals that there is no difference between two groups of farmers with regard to technological change. It indicates that the yield curve of Large farmers had shifted neutrally in relation to that of Small farmers. In the slope dummy, the co-efficient corresponding to capital flows emerged statistically significant. This implies that the structural difference between the two groups of farmers was caused with respect to the variable capital flows.

## YIELD GAP AND YIELD CONSTRAINTS

This section devotes to analyze the yield gap with respect to Large and Small farmers producing BG and GG of pulses in the study area. Further, it attempts to identify the main factors that act as constraints to the achievement of potential (maximum) yield at farm level in the study area. In the present study, yield gap II has been adopted. Yield gap II is defined as the difference between maximum yield and average yield obtained under farmer's conditions in the study area.

The observed yield gap at farm level between the potential and actual yield in the study area with respect to Large and Small farmers producing Black Gram and Green Gram of pulses was projected diagrammatically in Figures 5.1 and 5.2 respectively.

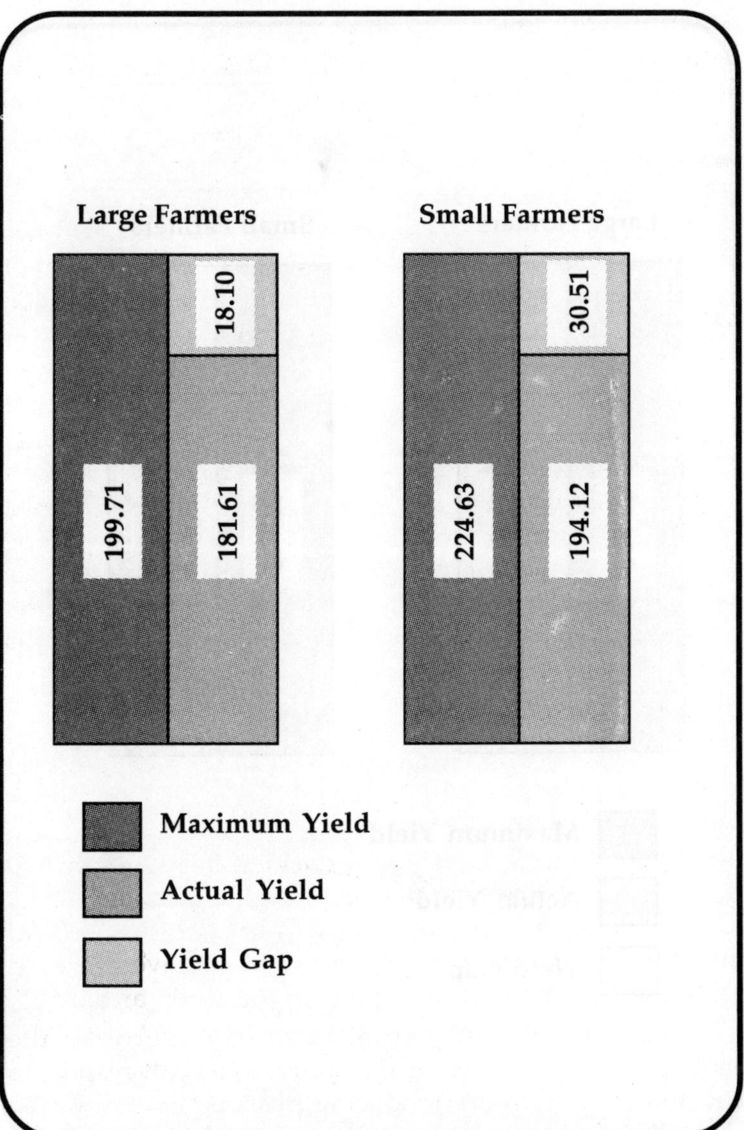


*Fig. 5.1:* Yield Gap Analysis of Pulses for Black Gram

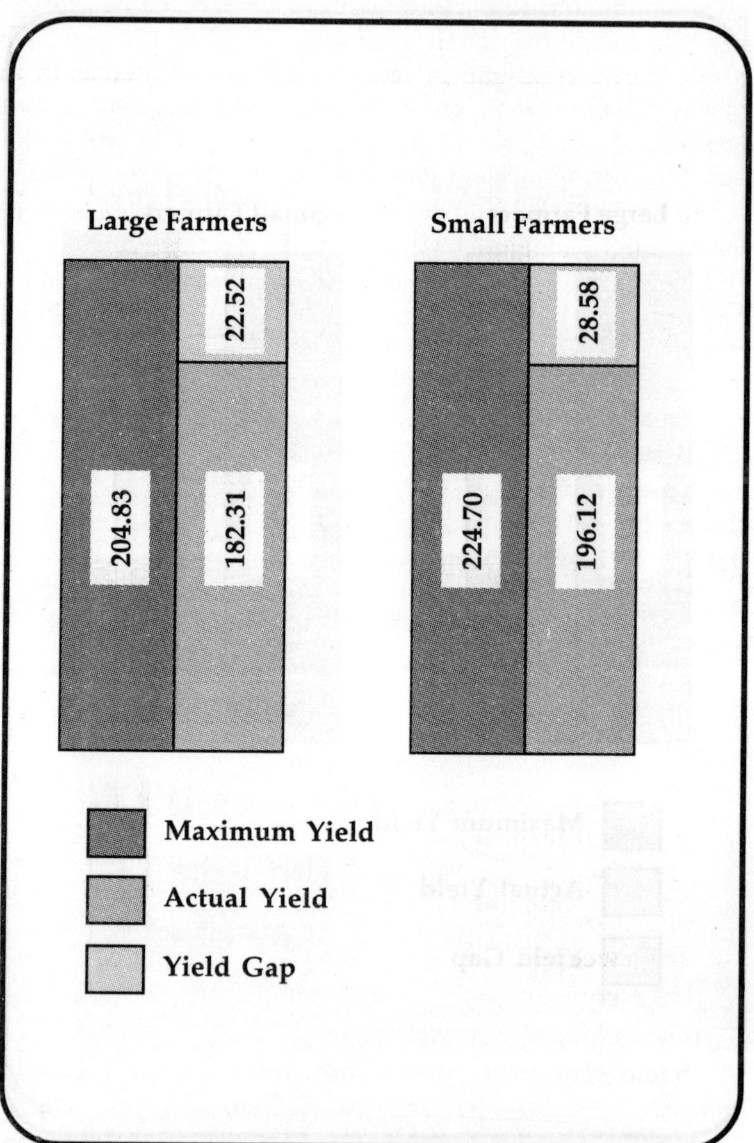


*Fig. 5.2:* **Yield Gap Analysis of Pulses for Green Gram**

In the case of Large farmers producing Black Gram of pulses in the study area, the maximum yield reaped was 199.71 kgs/acre while the actual yield was 181.61 kg per acre. This resulted in a yield gap of 18.10 kg per acre. Whereas in the case of Small farmers, the maximum yield obtained by them was 224.63 kgs per acre, while the actual yield was 194.12 kgs. This caused a yield gap of 30.51 kgs per acre.

It is observed that the farmers producing Green Gram, the resulted yield gap was found 22.52 kgs for Large farmers and 28.58 kgs for Small farmers. The maximum yield obtained by Large and Small farmers was 204.83 kgs and 224.70 kgs respectively. The actual yield was 182.31 kgs and 196.12 kgs for Large and Small farmers respectively.

Thus it is inferred from the analysis that the yield gap identified under Large farmers in both BG and GG pulses was Small compared to that of Small farmers producing both crops.

## YIELD CONSTRAINTS

The important yield constraints under farmer's condition are:

*(a)* bio-physical; and
*(b)* socio-economic.

Bio-physical constraints include:

*(i)* water shortage;
*(ii)* soil fertility;
*(iii)* problems of the soil
*(iv)* insects
*(v)* weeds
*(vi)* crop; and
*(vii)* cultural practices.

Socio-economic constraints comprise the following factors:

*(i)* credit;
*(ii)* non-availability of inputs (seed);

*(iii)* economic behaviour (risk aversion);

*(v)* knowledge; and

*(vi)* institutions; and

*(vii)* traditional methods.

Garrett's ranking technique was adopted to identify the main constraints to potential yield in the study area. The sample farmers were asked to rank the constraints faced by them as per priority. The order of merit assigned to each constraint by the respondents was converted into scores by using the formula

$$\text{Per cent position} = \frac{100\,(Rij\text{-}0.5)}{N_j} \qquad (5.4)$$

where

$R_{ij}$ = Rank given for the $i^{th}$ factor by $j^{th}$ farmer and

$N_j$ = Number of factors ranked by $j^{th}$ farmer.

The per cent position of each rank thus obtained was converted into scores by referring to Garrets ranking table. The scores of all respondents for each factor was then added together and divided by the number of respondents experiencing that particular constraint. The mean scores of each factor thus arrived at were arranged in a descending order and the corresponding ranks allotted.

The farmers cultivating pulses reported six factors among the various biological and socio-economic constraints as the major yield constraints which limited them from achieving the potential yield in the study area. It included water shortage, severity of disease and pest attacks, weeds, credit, non-availability of inputs (seeds) and traditional methods.

Table 5.7 highlights the yield constraints of Large farmers producing Black Gram of Pulses.

**Table 5.7: Yield Constraints of Large Farmers Producing Black Gram (BG)**

| Sl. No. | Constraints | Mean Score | Rank |
|---|---|---|---|
| 1. | Severity of disease and pest attacks | 64.75 | I |
| 2. | Water shortage | 58.64 | II |
| 3. | Inadequate credit facilities | 49.36 | III |
| 4. | Non- availability of input (Seeds) | 40.15 | IV |
| 5. | Weeds | 34.21 | V |
| 6. | Traditional methods | 31.15 | VI |

It is inferred from Table 5.7 that the severity of disease and pest attacks was ranked first followed by water shortage. Inadequate credit facilities were ranked third and non-availability of inputs (seeds) ranked fourth. Weeds and traditional methods were ranked fifth and sixth respectively.

The ranks assigned to the six identified factors for Small farmers are given in Table 5.8.

**Table 5.8: Yield Constraints of Small Farmers Producing Black Gram (BG)**

| Sl. No. | Constraints | Mean Score | Rank |
|---|---|---|---|
| 1. | Severity of disease and pest attacks | 61.24 | I |
| 2. | Water shortage | 52.63 | II |
| 3. | Inadequate credit facilities | 43.44 | III |
| 4. | Non- availability of input (Seeds) | 41.15 | IV |
| 5. | Weeds | 36.24 | V |
| 6. | Traditional methods | 31.49 | VI |

It is found from Table 5.8 that the severity of diseases and pest attacks was ranked first followed by water shortage. Inadequate credit facilities were ranked third and non-availability of inputs (seeds) ranked fourth. Weeds and traditional methods were ranked fifth and sixth.

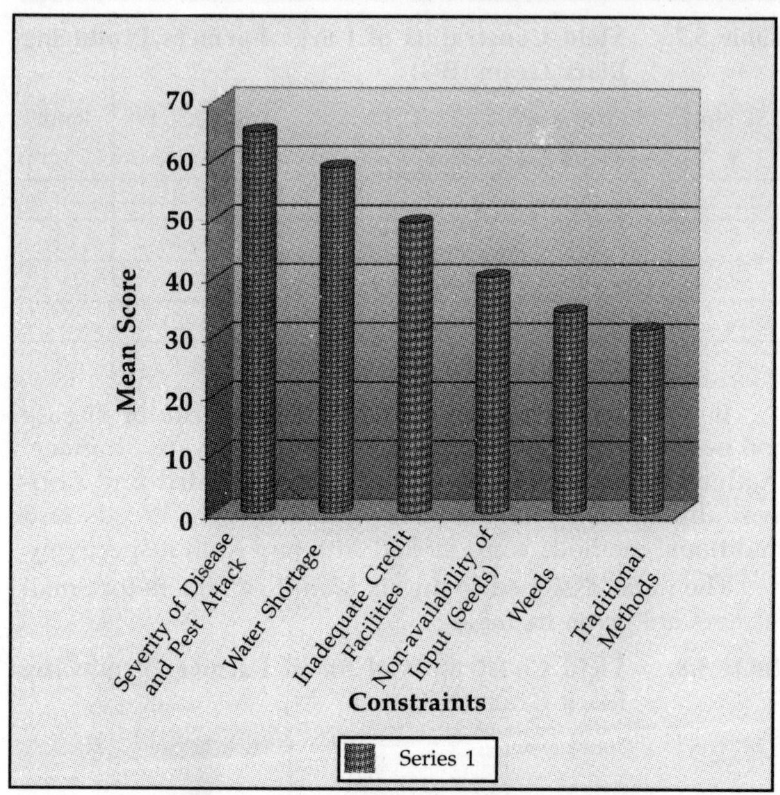


*Fig. 5.3:* **Yield Constraints of Large Farmers Producing Black Gram (BG)**

The mean score and ranks assigned to the six identified factors for Large farmers producing Green Gram (GG ) of pulses are presented in Table 5.9. (*See Table on page 114*)

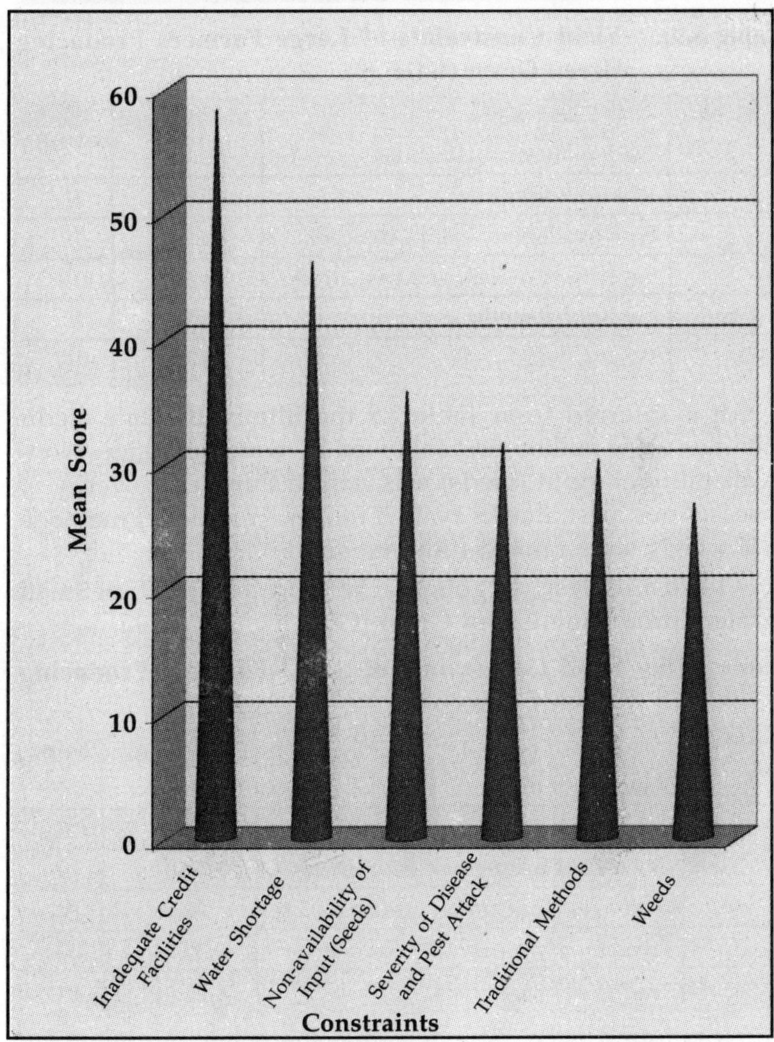


*Fig. 5.4:* **Yield Constraints of Large Farmers Producing Green Gram (GG)**

**Table 5.9: Yield Constraints of Large Farmers Producing Green Gram (GG)**

| Sl. No. | Constraints | Mean Score | Rank |
|---|---|---|---|
| 1. | Inadequate credit facilities | 58.15 | I |
| 2. | Water shortage | 45.99 | II |
| 3. | Non-availability of inputs (Seeds) | 35.64 | III |
| 4. | Severity of disease and pest attacks | 31.49 | IV |
| 5. | Traditional methods | 30.19 | V |
| 6. | Weeds | 26.62 | VI |

It is inferred from Table 5.9 that the inadequate credit facilities were ranked first followed by water shortage. Non-availability of input (seeds) was ranked third and severity of diseases and pest attacks ranked fourth. Traditional methods and weeds were ranked fifth and sixth.

Table 5.10 clearly highlights the yield constraints of Small farmers producing Green Gram (GG).

**Table 5.10: Yield Constraints of Small Farmers Producing Green Gram (GG)**

| Sl. No. | Constraints | Mean Score | Rank |
|---|---|---|---|
| 1. | Water shortage | 53.63 | I |
| 2. | Inadequate credit facilities | 45.15 | II |
| 3. | Severity of disease and pest attacks | 40.61 | III |
| 4. | Non-availability of inputs (Seeds) | 32.15 | IV |
| 5. | Weeds | 30.62 | V |
| 6. | Traditional methods | 22.64 | VI |

It is found from Table 5.10 that the water shortage was ranked first followed by inadequate credit facilities. Severity of disease and pest attacks was ranked third and non-availability of input (seeds) ranked fourth. Weeds and traditional methods were ranked fifth and sixth.

# CHAPTER 6

# Impact of Black Gram on Input Demand Elasticities, Supply Responsiveness, Labour Absorption and Factor Shares

The aim of this chapter is to estimate input demand elasticities and supply responsiveness for Large and Small farmers producing Black Gram (BG) and Green Gram (GG) of pulses in the study area. It also tries to examine the labour absorption capacity and returns to scale in BG and GG of pulses cultivation. For this, the conventional approaches using time series data, static and distributed lag models are replaced by profit function approach developed by Youtopoulos and Lau[1] to estimate simultaneously the profit function and input demand equations.

## THE ANALYTICAL FRAMEWORK

The profit function is inherently a cross-sectional approach.[2] The application of profit function approach is warranted only under conditions of price variations between farms at a point of time. Hence, special efforts were made during the survey to collect the details of price paid and received by the farmers.

The Normalised Profit Function derived from Cobb-Douglas Production Function was jointly estimated along with input demand functions with random disturbances. It was of the form:

$$\log \pi^* = \propto_0 + \beta^*_1 \log W + \beta^*_2 \log B + \beta^*_3 \log F + \beta^*_4 \log F + \propto_1^* \log A + \propto_2^* \log c + U \quad (6.1)$$

$$\left.\begin{array}{l} \dfrac{-WX_1}{\pi^*} = \beta_1^* + U_1 \\[2ex] \dfrac{-BX_2}{\pi^*} = \beta_1^* + U_2 \\[2ex] \dfrac{-FX_3}{\pi^*} = \beta_3^* + U_3 \\[2ex] \dfrac{-PX_4}{\pi^*} = \beta_4^* + U_4 \end{array}\right\} \quad (6.2)$$

where

$\pi^*$ = Real profit in rupees (that is total revenue minus total variable cost normalised by the price of output)

W = Real wages for labour

B = Real bullock pair day price

F = Real fertilizer price

P = Real pesticides price

A = Total area cultivated

C = Capital flows (calculated as the sum of depreciation, maintenance and opportunity cost of capital stock)

$X_1$ = Total labour man-days utilised

$X_2$ = Total bullock pair days

$X_3$ = Total quantity of fertilizer used and

$X_4$ = Total quantity of pesticides used.

The above equations (6.1) and (6.2) were jointly estimated by Zellner's[3] Seemingly Unrelated Regressions which gives asymptotically more efficient estimates than the production function estimated by ordinary least squares method. Since $\beta_i^*$ appears in both profit and demand functions, they were estimated jointly by imposing the conditions that $b_i^*$ is equal in two sets of equations.

## ANALYSIS OF BLACK GRAM (BG)

The estimated results of equation (6.1) and (6.2) for Large and Small farmers cultivating Black Gram of pulses are given in Table 6.1.

**Table 6.1: Estimated Results of Profit and Input Demand Function for Large and Small Farmers Producing Black Gram (BG)**

| Variables | Parameters | Estimates | |
|---|---|---|---|
| | | Large Farmers | Small Farmers |
| 1 | 2 | 3 | 4 |
| Intercept | $\propto_0$ | 3.8345 | 3.9261 |
| Log W | $\beta_1^*$ | -0.3575* (-3.1861) | -0.3162* (-2.9663) |
| Log B | $\beta_2^*$ | -0.0791* (-4.0181) | -0.0853* (-3.4636) |
| Log F | $\beta_3^*$ | -0.1962* (-2.3861) | -0.2216* (-3.7345) |
| Log P | $\beta_4^*$ | -0.1175* (-3.1865) | -0.1143* (-3.7543) |
| Log A | $\beta_1^*$ | 0.8175* (4.7435) | 0.7763* (3.4861) |
| Log C | $\beta_2^*$ | 0.1975* (2.6575) | 0.2615* (2.0148) |
| Labour demand | $\beta_1^*$ | -0.3575* (-3.1675) | -0.3149* (-2.9961) |

*(Contd...)*

| 1 | 2 | 3 | 4 |
|---|---|---|---|
| Bullock labour demand | $\beta_2^*$ | -0.0793* (-4.0182) | -0.0846* (-3.4565) |
| Fertilizer demand | $\beta_3^*$ | -0.1863* (-2.3761) | -0.2261* (-2.6861) |
| Pesticides demand | $\beta_4^*$ | -0.1121* (-3.7172) | -0.1273* (-3.7516) |

Figures in brackets represent t- value.

* Indicates significance at 5 per cent level.

## SUPPLY AND DEMAND ELASTICITIES

The own and cross price elasticities of demand for labour and elasticities with respect to supply of pulses were computed by using the formula given in Table 6.2.

**Table 6.2: Formula to Estimate Input Demand and Supply Elasticities Derived from COBB-Douglas Profit Function**

| Description | Formula |
|---|---|
| **(a) Input Demand Elasticities** | |
| (a) Own price elasticity of $X_1$ | $\beta_1^*-1$ |
| (b) Cross price elasticity for $X_1$ with respect to real price of $X_1$ | $\beta_j^*$ |
| (c) Variable input $X_1$ with respect to fixed factor, $Z_j$ | $\propto_1^*$ |
| (d) Demand elasticity of $X_1$ with respect to output price | $-\Sigma\beta_i^*+1$ |
| **(b) Supply Elasticities** | |
| (a) Supply elasticity with respect to output price | $-\sum_{i=1}^{n}\beta_j^*$ |
| (b) Supply elasticity with respect to real price of in the variable input $X_1$ | $\beta_j^*$ |
| (c) Supply elasticity with respect to fixed input $Z_j$ | $\propto_1^*$ |

*Source:* Lawrence J. Lau and Pan A Yotopoulos "Profit, Supply and Factor Demand Functions", *American Journal of Agricultural Economics*, Vol.54, No. 1, February 1972, p. 17.

Table 6.3 shows the own and cross price elasticities of demand for labour for Large and Small farmers cultivating BG of pulses.

**Table 6.3: Own and Cross Price Elasticities of Demand for Labour for Large and Small Farmers Cultivating Black Gram (BG)**

| Sl. No. | Variables | Labour Demand | |
|---|---|---|---|
| | | Large Farmers | Small Farmers |
| 1. | Pulses price | 1.7503 | 1.7374 |
| 2. | Real Wage | -1.3575 | -1.3162 |
| 3. | Real Bullock Pair price | -0.0791 | -0.0853 |
| 4. | Real Fertilizer price | -0.1962 | -0.2216 |
| 5. | Real Pesticide price | -0.1175 | -0.1143 |
| 6. | Land | 0.8175 | 0.7763 |
| 7. | Capital | 0.1975 | 0.2615 |

*Source:* Computed Data.

From Table 6.3, the labour demand elasticities for Large and Small farmers of pulses (BG) with respect to own prices were 1.7503 and 1.7374 respectively Changes in pulses prices for Large and Small farmers appeared to have a significant effect on the demand for labour in the study area. A 10 per cent increase in pulses (BG) price of Large and Small farmers was found to ensure a more than 10 per cent rise in the demand for labour.

The elasticities indicated that a 10 per cent increase in the real wage would induce the farmers to reduce labour employment by 13.575 per cent in the case of Large farmers and 13.162 per cent in the case of Small farmers. This implies that wage rate is also one of the factors that significantly affects farm employment of pulses cultivators' particularly Black Gram cultivation.

The elasticities of Large and Small farmers demand for labour in relation to land were 0.8175 and 0.7763 per cent respectively. In the case of capital, the respective elasticities were 0.1975 and 0.2615. This indicates that an increase in the area of pulse farmers had a more favourable impact on the demand for Large farmers than on Small farmers.

The study shows that Large farmers had the capacity to absorb an increased amount of labour more than Small farmers producing Black Gram of pulses.

Table 6.4 shows the demand for variable inputs with respect to own prices for Large and Small farmers producing Black Gram of pulses.

**Table 6.4: Demand for Variable Inputs with Respect to Their Own Prices for Large and Small Farmers Producing Black Gram (BG)**

| Sl. No. | Particulars | Elasticities | |
|---|---|---|---|
| | | Large Farmers | Small Farmers |
| 1. | Demand for labour with respect to real wage | -1.3575 | -1.3162 |
| 2. | Demand for bullock labour with respect to real bullock price | -1.0791 | -1.0853 |
| 3. | Demand for fertilizer with respect to real fertilizer price | -1.1962 | -1.2216 |
| 4. | Demand for pesticides with respect to real pesticides price | -1.1175 | -1.1143 |

*Source:* Computed Data.

It is revealed from Table 6.4 that a 10 per cent increase in the price of variable inputs in Black Gram, namely labour fertilizer, pesticides and bullock labour, was accompanied by 13.575 per cent, -1.0791 per cent, 10.853 per cent and 11.962 per cent in their respective demands in the case of Large farmers. In the case of Small farmers, it was 13.162 per cent, 10.853 per cent, 12.216 per cent and 11.143 per cent in the demands of the respective variable inputs. This indicates that the demand for variable inputs with respect to their own price was highly elastic for both Large and Small farmers producing pulses. That is, a 10 per cent increase in the price of the variable inputs was followed by a more than 10 per cent fall in their demand. Adulavidhaye[4] et.al and Subramaniyan[5] arrived at similar conclusions in their studies.

Among the price of variable inputs, real wage appeared to be relatively the most important factor of production, affecting agricultural employment to a considerable extent.

The own and cross price elasticities of demand for variable inputs with respect to Large and Small farmers cultivating Black Gram of pulses are presented in Table 6.5.

**Table 6.5: Own and Cross Price Elasticities of Demand for Variable Inputs for Large and Small Farmers Producing Black Gram (BG)**

| Particulars | Price of Labour | Price of Bullock Labour | Price of Fertilizer | Price of Pesticide |
|---|---|---|---|---|
| **Large Farmers** | | | | |
| Demand for Labour | -1.3575 | -0.0791 | -0.1962 | -0.1175 |
| Demand for Bullock pairs | -0.3575 | -1.0791 | -0.1962 | -0.1175 |
| Demand for fertiliser | -0.3575 | -0.0791 | -1.1962 | -0.1175 |
| Demand for pesticides | -0.3575 | -0.0791 | -0.1962 | -1.1175 |
| **Small Farmers** | | | | |
| Demand for Labour | -1.3162 | -0.0853 | -0.2216 | -0.1143 |
| Demand for Bullock pairs | -0.3162 | -1.0853 | -0.2216 | -0.1143 |
| Demand for fertiliser | -0.3162 | -0.0853 | -1.2216 | -0.1143 |
| Demand for pesticides | -0.3162 | -0.0853 | -0.2216 | -1.1143 |

*Source:* Computed Data.

Table 6.5 shows that the own and cross price elasticities of demand for variable inputs with respect to Large and Small farmers producing Black Gram of pulses were negative and indicates that they were complements rather than substitutes.

In sum, though cross price elasticities among the variable inputs were low, indicating a weak relationship, these factors were observed to be complements rather than substitutes for both Large and Small farmers producing Black Gram of pulses.

The own and cross price elasticities of output supply for Large and Small farmers producing Black Gram of pulses are given in Table 6.6.

**Table 6.6: Own and Cross Price Elasticities of Output Supply for Large and Small Farmers Producing Black Gram (BG)**

| Sl. No. | Variables | Output Supply | |
|---|---|---|---|
| | | Large Farmers | Small Farmers |
| 1. | Black Gram price | 0.7291 | 0.7314 |
| 2. | Real Wage | -0.3575 | -0.3162 |
| 3. | Real Bullock Pair Price | -0.0791 | -0.0853 |
| 4. | Real Fertilizer price | -0.1962 | -0.2216 |
| 5. | Real Pesticide price | -0.1175 | -0.1143 |
| 6. | Land | 0.8175 | 0.7763 |
| 7. | Capital | 0.1975 | 0.2615 |

*Source:* Computed Data.

It is inferred from Table 6.6 that the output supply elasticities for Large and Small farmers producing pulses with respect to own price in BG were 0.7291 and 0.7314 respectively. In other words, '*ceteris paribus*', a 10 per cent increase in price of pulses for Large and Small farmers would respectively increase their output supply by 7.291 per cent and 7.314 per cent. This would imply that the Large and Small farmers were comparatively equally responsive to changes in price of pulses.

This indicates that the manipulation of pulses price of Small and Large farmers may be considered an effective policy tool to increase the output supply of Black Gram.

## INDIRECT ESTIMATES OF PRODUCTION ELASTICITIES

The indirect estimates of production elasticities for Large and Small farmers producing Black Gram are obtained from the 'real' profit function derived by Lau and Yotopulos. The formulae for computing indirect estimates are given below.

$$\propto_j = \propto_j^* (1-\mu^*)^{-1} \qquad j = 1, 2, \text{——} m$$

$$\beta_j = -\beta_j^* (1-\mu^*)^{-1} \qquad j = 1,2, \text{——} n$$

$$\mu^* = \sum_{j=1}^{n} \beta_j^* \qquad (6.3)$$

where

$\mu_j$ = Indirect estimate of production

$b_j$ = Indirect estimate of production elasticities of the variable inputs

$\mu_j^*$ = Co-efficient of fixed inputs in the profit function;

$b_j^*$ = Co-efficient of variable inputs in the profit function

The computed results of direct and indirect estimates of production elasticities are shown in Table 6.7.

**Table 6.7: Direct and Indirect Estimates of Production Elasticities**

| Variables | Large Farmers | | Small Farmers | |
|---|---|---|---|---|
| | Direct | Indirect | Direct | Indirect |
| Human Labour | 0.2819* (3.1861) | 0.2043 | 0.2761* (3.1845) | 0.1820 |
| Bullock Labour | 0.0079 (1.0371) | 0.0452 | 0.0173 (0.7319) | 0.0491 |
| Fertilizer | 0.2174* (2.6514) | 0.1121 | 0.1821* (3.1821) | 0.1275 |
| Pesticides | 0.1141 (1.3341) | 0.0671 | 0.0861* (2.1861) | 0.0678 |
| Land | 0.3861* (4.1961) | 0.4671 | 0.3661* (3.1772) | 0.4468 |
| Capital | 0.1139* (2.7861) | 0.1128 | 0.1735* (3.7262) | 0.1505 |
| Sum of elasticities | 1.0971 | | 1.0981 | |
| $R^2$ | 0.7961 | | 0.7961 | |

Figures in brackets are t-Value

* Indicates significance at 5 per cent level.

It could be observed from Table 6.7 that the indirect estimate of production elasticities of land in Black Gram was the highest (0.4671), followed by human labour (0.2043), capital (0.1128) and fertilizer (0.1121) for Large farmers. In the case of Small farmers, the indirect estimate of production elasticities of land was found to be the highest (0.4468), followed by human labour (0.1820), capital (0.1505) and fertilizer (0.1275).

It is evident from the indirect estimates that the share of land in the total output was the highest, which is 0.4671 and 0.4468 per cent respectively for Large and Small farmers cultivating BG of pulses. Comparing these two farmers, Large farmers had a greater share of land than Small farmers. Share of human labour in output was 0.2043 per cent for Large farmers. The share of capital was higher for Small farmers than for Large farmers.

The share of fertilizer in output was found to be higher for Small farmers than for the Large farmers. The share of pesticides and the bullock labour in total output was low for both Large and Small farmers.

## ANALYSIS OF GREEN GRAM (GG)

The results of joint estimation of profit function (6.1) and input demand functions (6.2) for Large and Small farmers cultivating Green Gram of pulses are given in Table 6.8.

**Table 6.8: Estimated Results of Profit and Input Demand Functions for Large and Small Farmers Producing Green Gram (GG)**

| Variables | Parameters | Estimates | |
|---|---|---|---|
| | | Large Farmers | Small Farmers |
| 1 | 2 | 3 | 4 |
| Intercept | $\alpha_0$ | 3.0922 | 2.9561 |
| log W | $\beta_1^{*}$ | -0.3426*<br>(-3.1261) | -0.3161*<br>(-2.8861) |

*(Contd...)*

| 1 | 2 | 3 | 4 |
|---|---|---|---|
| log B | $\beta_2^*$ | -0.0561* (-2.4261) | -0.1140* (-2.6215) |
| log F | $\beta_3^*$ | -0.2861* (-3.1819) | -0.2161* (-4.6861) |
| log P | $\beta_4^*$ | -0.0819* (-2.6819) | -0.0961* (-2.1961) |
| log A | $\beta_1^*$ | 0.8161* (2.6929) | 0.7515* (3.4365) |
| log C | $\beta_2^*$ | 0.2361* (3.7426) | 0.2961* (2.6118) |
| Labour Demand | $\beta_1^*$ | -0.3361* (-3.1262) | -0.3199* (-2.8818) |
| Bullock Labour demand | $\beta_2^*$ | -0.0491* (-2.4515) | -0.1121* (-2.6218) |
| Fertilizer Demand | $\beta_3^*$ | -0.2861* (-3.1861) | -0.1929* (-4.6835) |
| Pesticides Demand | $\beta_4^*$ | -0.0819* (-2.6929) | -0.0962* (-2.1862) |

Figures in brackets represent t-value.

* Indicates significance at 5 per cent level.

## OWN AND CROSS PRICE ELASTICITIES OF DEMAND FOR LABOUR

The computed results of own and cross price elasticities of demand for labour for Large and Small farmers cultivating GG of pulses are given in Tale 6.9. (*See Table on next page*)

From Table 6.9, the labour demand elasticities for Large farmers and Small farmers of pulses in Green Gram with respect to own Price were 1.7667 and 1.7425 respectively. Changes in pulses Price for Large and Small farmers appeared to have a significant effect on the demand for labour in the study area. A 10 per cent increase in pulses Price of Large and Small farmers was found to ensure a more than 10 per cent rise in the demand for labour.

**Table 6.9: Own and Cross Price Elasticities of Demand for Labour for Large and Small Farmers Producing Green gram (GG)**

| Sl. No. | Variables | Labour Demand | |
|---|---|---|---|
| | | Large Farmers | Small Farmers |
| 1. | Pulses prices | 1.7667 | 1.7425 |
| 2. | Real Wage | -1.3426 | -1.3161 |
| 3. | Real Bullock Pair Price | -0.0561 | -0.1142 |
| 4. | Real Fertilizer Price | -0.2861 | -0.2161 |
| 5. | Real Pesticide Price | -0.0819 | -0.0961 |
| 6. | Land | 0.8161 | 0.7515 |
| 7. | Capital | 0.2361 | 0.2961 |

*Source:* Computed Data.

The elasticities indicated that a 10 per cent increase in the real wage would induce the farmers to reduce labour employment by 13.426 per cent in the case of Large farmers and 13.161 per cent in the case of Small farmers. This implies that wage rate is also one of the factors that significantly affect farm employment of pulses cultivators.

The elasticities of Large and Small farmer demand for labour in relation to land were 0.8161 and 0.7515 per cent respectively. In the case of capital, the respective elasticities were 0.2361 and 0.2961. This indicates that an increase in the area of pulses cultivating farmers had a more favourable impact on the demand for Large farmers than on Small farmers.

The study shows that Large farmers had the capacity to absorb an increased amount of labour more than Small farmers producing pulses.

Table 6.10 highlights the demand for variable inputs with respect to own Price for Large and Small farmers cultivating Green gram of pulses.

**Table 6.10: Demand for Variable Inputs with Respect to Their Own Price for Large and Small Farmers Producing Green Gram (GG)**

| Sl. No. | Particulars | Elasticities | |
|---|---|---|---|
| | | Large Farmers | Small Farmers |
| 1. | Demand for labour with respect to real wage | -1.3426 | -1.3161 |
| 2. | Demand for bullock labour with respect to real bullock price | -1.0561 | -1.1142 |
| 3. | Demand for fertiliser with respect to real fertiliser price | -1.2861 | -1.2161 |
| 4. | Demand for pesticides with respect to real pesticides price | -1.0819 | -1.0961 |

*Source:* Computed Data.

It is revealed from Table 6.10 that a 10 per cent increase in the prices of variable inputs in traditional crop, namely labour, fertilizer, pesticides and bullock labour was accompanied by 13.426 per cent, 10.561 per cent, 12.861 per cent and 10.819 per cent in their respective demand in the case of Large farmers. In the case of Small farmers, it was 13.161 per cent, 11.142 per cent, 12.161 per cent and 10.961 per cent in the demands of the respective variable inputs. This indicates that the demands for variable inputs with respect to their own prices were highly elastic for both Large and Small farmers producing pulses. That is, a 10 per cent increase in the prices of the variable inputs was followed by a more than 10 per cent fall in their demand.

Among the prices of variable inputs, real wage appeared to be elastically the most important factor of production, affecting agricultural employment to a considerable extent.

## OWN AND CROSS PRICE ELASTICITIES OF DEMAND FOR VARIABLE INPUTS

The own and cross price elasticities of demand for variable inputs are given in Table 6.11.

**Table 6.11: Own and Cross Price Elasticities of Demand for Variable Inputs for Large and Small Farmers Producing Green Gram (GG)**

| Particulars | Price of Labour | Price of Bullock Labour | Price of Fertiliser | Price of Pesticide |
|---|---|---|---|---|
| | **Large Farmers** | | | |
| Demand for Labour | -1.3426 | -0.0561 | -0.2861 | -0.0819 |
| Demand for Bullock pairs | -0.3426 | -1.0561 | -0.2861 | -0.0819 |
| Demand for fertilizer | -0.3426 | -0.0561 | -1.2861 | -0.0819 |
| Demand for pesticides | -0.3426 | -0.0561 | -0.2861 | -1.0819 |
| | **Small Farmers** | | | |
| Demand for Labour | -1.3161 | -0.1142 | -0.2161 | -0.0961 |
| Demand for Bullock pairs | -0.3161 | -1.1142 | -0.2161 | -0.0961 |
| Demand for fertilizer | -0.3161 | -0.1142 | -1.2161 | -0.0961 |
| Demand for pesticides | -0.3161 | -0.1142 | -0.2161 | -1.0961 |

*Source:* Computed Data.

Table 6.11 shows that the cross elasticities of the variable inputs for Large and Small farmers producing pulses in Green Gram were negative and indicates that they were complements rather than substitutes.

In sum, though the cross Price elasticities among the variable inputs were low, indicating a weak relationship, these factors were observed to be complements rather than substitutes for both Large and Small farmers producing pulses.

## OWN AND CROSS PRICE ELASTICITIES OF OUTPUT SUPPLY GREEN GRAM (GG)

Table 6.12 shows the own and cross Price elasticities of output supply for Large and Small farmers.

**Table 6.12: Own and Cross Price Elasticities of Output Supply for Large and Small Farmers Producing Green Gram (GG)**

| Sl. No. | Variables | Output Supply | |
|---|---|---|---|
| | | Large Farmers | Small Farmers |
| 1. | Pulses Price | 0.7667 | 0.7425 |
| 2. | Real Wage | -0.3426 | -0.3161 |
| 3. | Real Bullock Pair Price | -0.0561 | -0.1172 |
| 4. | Real Fertiliser Price | -0.2861 | -0.2161 |
| 5. | Real Pesticide Price | -0.0819 | -0.0961 |
| 6. | Land | 0.8161 | 0.7515 |
| 7. | Capital | 0.2361 | 0.2961 |

*Source:* Computed Data.

It is inferred from Table 6.12 that, the output supply elasticities for Large and Small farmers producing pulses in Green Gram with respect to own Price were 0.7667 and 0.7425 respectively. In other words, *'ceteris paribus'*, a 10 per cent increase in Price of pulses for Large and Small farmers would respectively increase their output supply by 7.667 per cent and 7.425 per cent. This would imply that the Large and Small farmers were by comparison, equally responsive to changes in the Price of pulses.

This indicates that the manipulation of pulses Price of Small and Large farmers may be considered an effective policy tool to increase the output supply of pulses.

## INDIRECT ESTIMATES OF PRODUCTION ELASTICITIES

The indirect estimates of production elasticities for Large and Small farmers cultivating GG of pulses by using the formula (6.3) and the results are presented in Tale 6.13.

**Table 6.13: Direct and Indirect Estimates of Production Elasticities**

| Variables | Large Farmers | | Small Farmers | |
|---|---|---|---|---|
| | Direct | Indirect | Direct | Indirect |
| Human Labour | 0.2762* (3.2161) | 0.1939 | 0.2561* (3.6516) | 0.1814 |
| Bullock Labour | 0.0471 (0.0671) | 0.0318 | 0.0376 (0.0975) | 0.0655 |
| Fertilizer | 0.0938* (2.7141) | 0.1619 | 0.2070* (2.7861) | 0.1240 |
| Pesticides | 0.0112 (0.3711) | 0.0464 | 0.0402 (1.0210) | 0.0552 |
| Land | 0.3871* (3.9241) | 0.4619 | 0.3371* (3.7261) | 0.4313 |
| Capital | 0.1068* (2.7147) | 0.1336 | 0.1415 (4.1621) | 0.1699 |
| Sum of elasticities | 0.9222 | | 1.0195 | |
| $R^2$ | 0.8169 | | 0.8091 | |

Figures in brackets are t-Value

* Indicates significance at 5 per cent level.

From Table 6.13, it could be observed that the indirect estimate of production elasticities of land in Green Gram was the highest (0.4619) followed by human labour (0.1939), capital (0.1336) and fertilizer (0.1619) for Large farmers. In the case of Small farmers, the indirect estimate of production elasticities of land was found to be the highest (0.4313), followed by human labour (0.1814), capital (0.1699) and fertilizer (0.1240).

It is evident from the indirect estimates that the share of land in the total output was the highest, which is 0.4619 and 0.4313 per cent respectively for Large and Small farmers growing pulses. Comparing these two farmers, Large farmers had a greater share of land than Small farmers. Share of human labour in output was 0.1893 for Large farmers. The share of capital was higher for Small farmers than for Large farmers.

The share of fertilizer in output was found to be higher for Small farmers than for the Large farmers. The share of pesticides and bullock labour in total output was low for both Large and Small farmers.

## IMPACT OF BLACK GRAM (BG) ON FACTOR SHARES

This section discusses the impact of Black Gram on factor shares, nature of factor bias and factor shares in total income, through profit function analysis.

Factor combination and factor shares in agriculture depend on a number of factors such as the resource endowments of the region, cropping pattern, level of technology used, factor Price and government policy. Distribution of factor shares and their changes over time and space are important in the context of economic growth and social justice.[6] Technical change in terms of introducing Black Gram seeds is one of the major forces leading to changes in output, employment and functional income distribution.[7] Technical change is labour saving, labour-neutral or labour-using depending on whether the labour share in total cost decrease, remaining constant or increases at constant factor Price.[8]

Most researchers have concentrated on the effect of farm size on efficiency as measured by absolute productivity differences in gross returns in irrigated agriculture.[9]

Efficiency of agricultural operation can be deduced from the combinations of factors of production in farm operations.[10] Technological change has led to considerable increase in agricultural output and income.[11]

The study would help in understanding the impact of cropping pattern, on the changes in factor shares. The researcher seeks to examine in detail, the estimation of factor shares in Indian agriculture with particular reference to shift from Green Gram (GG) to Black Gram (BG).

## Measurement of Production Elasticities

The Unit Output Price (UOP) profit function developed by L.J. Lau and P.A. Yotopoulos[12] has been used here to identify the important factors of production which influence productivity.

The technical bias is measured as changes in output elasticities. The production elasticities measured on the basis of production function are found to be biased and inconsistent. The profit function helps to overcome the problem of simultaneous equation bias in the estimation of production elasticities of production function. The estimated parameters of profit functions may be used to derive elasticities of production function indirectly.[13]

The estimated results of equation (6.1) and (6.2) for BG and GG of pulses cultivating farmers are given in Table 6.14.

**Table 6.14: Estimated Results of Profit and Input Demand Function for BG and GG of Pulses Producting Farmers**

| Variables | Parameters | Estimates | |
|---|---|---|---|
| | | BG | GG |
| 1 | 2 | 3 | 4 |
| Intercept | $\alpha_0$ | 3.6620 | 2.9864 |
| Log W | $\beta_1$* | -0.3360*<br>(-4.5020) | -0.3116*<br>(-4.1670) |
| Log B | $\beta_2$* | -0.0793*<br>(-5.1616) | -0.0958*<br>(-2.6165) |
| Log F | $\beta_3$* | -0.1931*<br>(-3.6720) | -0.2165*<br>(-3.6518) |
| Log P | $\beta_4$* | -0.1011*<br>(-2.9214) | -0.0863*<br>(-2.8614) |
| Log A | $\alpha_1$ | 0.7942*<br>(6.1248) | 0.7528*<br>(4.3212) |
| Log C | $\alpha_2$ | 0.2116*<br>(3.6621) | 0.2516*<br>(6.1811) |

*(Contd...)*

| 1 | 2 | 3 | 4 |
|---|---|---|---|
| Labour Demand | $\beta_1$* | -0.3360* (-4.5020) | -0.3116* (-4.1670) |
| Bullock Labour Demand | $\beta_2$* | -0.0793* (-5.1616) | -0.0958* (-2.6165) |
| Fertilizer Demand | $\beta_3$* | -0.1931* (-3.6720) | -0.2165* (-3.6518) |
| Pesticides Demand | $\beta_4$* | -0.1011* (-2.9214) | -0.0863* (-2.8614) |

The indirect estimates of production elasticities derived from the Cobb-Douglas production function by using the results in Table 6.14 are furnished in Table 6.15.

**Table 6.15: Indirect Estimate of Production Elasticities from the COBB-Douglas Profit Function**

| Inputs | Parameters | Estimates of Production Elasticities | |
|---|---|---|---|
| | | BG | GG |
| Human Labour | $a_1$ | 0.1966 | 0.1822 |
| Bullock Labour | $a_2$ | 0.0464 | 0.0560 |
| Fertilizer | $a_3$ | 0.1130 | 0.1266 |
| Pesticides | $a_4$ | 0.0591 | 0.0505 |
| Land | $a_5$ | 0.4646 | 0.4402 |
| Capital | $a_6$ | 0.1238 | 0.1471 |

From Table 6.15, it is observed that the partial elasticities of production function $a_1$ to $a_6$ with constant returns to scale are the factor shares in output. The share of land is found to be the maximum for both the varieties. There is a slight difference between two crops regarding share of land in output. The human labour share in output is found to be higher for BG than GG of pulses. Therefore, the share of human labour has increased substantially as one move from GG to BG cultivation. It indicates the efficiency gain regarding labour found in BG cultivation, that is, a given amount of output can be produced with less amounts of human labourers under

BG cultivation. In the case of capital, BG cultivation requires less of capital inputs than GG cultivation. Therefore, the share of capital in BG is less compared to GG of pulses.

**Nature of Factors Bias and Factor Shares in Total Income**

This section attempts to analyse the nature of factor bias due to change in cultivating BG of pulses which may be labour-using or capital-using accordingly as the marginal rate of substitution of capital for labour increases or decreases.

Binswanger[14] in his study, "The Management of Technical Change Biases with many Factors of Production", reveals a slightly modified version and defines factors bias in terms of factor shares in total cost. In the present study, Binswanger's modified version has been used to examine the nature of factor biases due to change in the introduction of BG that is due to the shift from Traditional and New Technology in the study area. The shifting of area from GG and BG is labour saving, labour neutral or labour using, as the labour share in total cost decreases remains constant or increases respectively. The biases of factors of production are measured using the Binswanger's of the following empirical model.

$$B_i = \frac{(a_i)_{BG} - (a_i)_{GG}}{(a_i)_{GG}}$$

where,

$a_i$ = Output elasticity of $i^{th}$ factor,

BG = Black Gram and

GG = Green Gram

As per definition of the concept, that is, $i^{th}$ input saving neutral or input using, if the value $B_i < 0$, $B_i = 0$, $B_i > 0$, accordingly.

**Nature of Bias**

The nature of technical bias in BG and GG of pulses cultivation is measured with the help of the production elasticities presented in Table 6.15 and the result is furnished in Table 6.16.

**Table 6.16: Nature of Technical Bias in Black Gram (BG) of Pulses Cultivation**

| Cultivation | Factor | Proportionate Change in Output Elasticity | Nature of Technical Bias |
|---|---|---|---|
| BG Versus GG | Human labour | 0.0144 | Human Labour using |
| | Bullock Labour | -0.0096 | Fertilizer saving |
| | Fertilizer | -0.0136 | Pesticides saving |
| | Pesticides | 0.0086 | Bullock Pair using |
| | Land | 0.0244 | Land Using |
| | Capital | -0.0233 | Capital Saving |

Table 6.16 reveals that BG of pulses cultivation is biased in favour of human labour, pesticides and land and it against for bullock labour, fertilizer and capital. This shows the need for intensive use of human labour, pesticides and land rather than fertilizer and other variable inputs in the BG of pulses cultivation. Thus, the cultivation of BG of pulses leads to a considerable using a labour in the study area. The BG of pulses cultivation reduces the problem of unemployment in the agricultural sector, particularly in the study area.

## Absolute Factor Shares in Total Income

The absolute factor shares rather than relative factor shares provide a better perspective on functional distribution problem. The change in absolute factor shares in total income could be measured by multiplying total incomes by production elasticities. The calculated value of percentage change in absolute factor shares is presented in Table 6.17. (*See Table on next page*)

This percentage change in absolute factor shares in Table 6.17 reveals that all the factors of production except capital stand to gain absolute terms due to the shift to BG cultivation. This may be the main reason for shifting the area to BG from GG cultivation in the study area. The percentage gain is the maximum for pesticides under BG of pulses cultivation.

**Table 6.17: Percentage Change in Absolute Factor Shares**

| Cultivation | Factor of Production | Absolute Factor Share per Acre (in Rupees) | | Percentage Change in Absolute Factor Share |
|---|---|---|---|---|
| | | BG | GG | |
| BG Versus GG of Pulses | Human labour | 2699.21 | 2315.41 | 21.08 |
| | Bullock Labour | 683.18 | 605.22 | 11.46 |
| | Fertilizer | 1665.21 | 1664.22 | 0.109 |
| | Pesticides | 872.61 | 664.21 | 23.69 |
| | Land | 6842.22 | 5862.22 | 14.51 |
| | Capital | 1816.21 | 1856.15 | 2.22 |

## COMPARATIVE ANALYSIS OF BG AND GG FARMERS' GROUPS

This section attempts to compare the supply responsiveness, input demand elasticities and factor shares of BG and GG.

### Demand for Labour

It is observed from the analysis that both Large and Small farmers of BG group have a much more responsiveness for absorption of labour with respect to output price compared to the farmers of uneducated group in the study area. This shows that BG farmers have the capacity to absorb an increased amount of labour than GG farmers in the study area.

The elasticities of real wage indicate a significant effect on the demand for labour in pulses production. And it is found to be higher for BG farmers than for GG farmers. A 10 per cent increase in real wage rate caused nearly 13.36 per cent and 13.02 per cent reduction in employment of labour for BG and GG farmers respectively.

### Supply Responsiveness

The output supply elasticities for BG farmers with respect to own price was found to be high (more than 80 per cent) compared to GG farmers (nearly 72 per cent). It is inferred from the analysis that BG farmers are comparatively more responsive to changes in output price than GG farmers.

Regarding own and cross price elasticities of demand for variable inputs, the BG farmers are found to be more sensitive than GG farmers in the study area. In both groups, the cross price elasticities are negative and low, indicating that they are complements rather than substitutes. Further, it may be observed that a given change in any of the exogenous variable in inputs demand is symmetric because of interest assumption of unit elasticity of substitutes among input pairs in the Cobb-Douglas production function.

**Returns to Scale**

The magnitude of the indirect estimate of the production function elasticities is found to be quite logical and consistent with the *a priori* expectations of economic theory for both cases. It is noticed that the dominance of production elasticity with respect to land is high in the case of BG farmers than in the case of GG farmers. In both the cases, labour is the next important factor in pulses production in the study area. The indirect estimates for the two groups reveal the prevalence of constant returns to scale. This finding rules out the policy of consolidation of holdings in the study area.

**Factor Shares**

The share of land is found to be the more maximum for BG than for GG in the study area.

The share of human labour had increased from 0.1822 to 0.1966 indicating efficiency gain in production with respect to labour under pulse cultivation.

BG of pulses cultivation requires more capital for a given output as compared to GG cultivation.

BG of pulses cultivation is biased in favour of human labour, pesticides and land is against, for fertilizers, bullock pair and capital. The adoption of BG of pulses cultivation had increased employment opportunities in the agricultural sector.

The absolute share of all factors except capital had increased with the adoption of BG of pulses cultivation. The farmers in the study who had to change their pulses cultivation of BG stood to gain. The absolute share was the maximum for pesticides under BG of the cultivation.

## REFERENCES


1. A. Yotopoulos and L.J. Lau, "Resource Use in Agriculture Application of the Production Function to Selected Countries", *Food Research Institute Studies*, 17 (1) 1979, pp. 1-119.
2. John Quiggin and Anh Bui-Lau, 'The use of Cross Sectional Estimates of Profit Functions for Tests of Relative Efficiency: A Critical Review", *Australian Journal of Agricultural Economics*, Vol. 28, No. 1, April 1984, pp. 44-45.
3. Arnold Zellner. "An Efficient Method of Estimating Seemingly Unrelated Regression and Test of Aggregation Bias", *Journal of American Statistical Association*, Vol. 57, No. 2, June 1962, pp. 348-375.
4. Kamphol Adulavidhaya, et.al., 'A Micro Economic Analysis of the Agriculture of Jhailand" (Eds) *Food Research Institute Studies*, Vol. XVII, No. 2, 1979, pp. 79-86.
5. G. Subramaniyan, "Labour Demand and Supply Responsiveness of Cotton in Madurai district", *Indian Journal of Agricultural Economics*, Vol. 41, No. 2, April-June, 1986, pp. 155-163.
6. M.V. George, N.J. Kurien and C. Chandra Mohan, "Factor Shares in Indian Agriculture: Temporal and Spatial Variations and Their Implications", *Indian Journal of Agricultural Economics*, Vol. XXXVIII, No. 3, July-September, 1983, p. 399.
7. M.R. Alshi, P. Kumar and V.C. Mathur, "Technological Change and Factor Shares in Cotton Production: A Case Study of Ashola Cotton Farms", *Indian Journal of Agricultural Economics*, Vol. XXXVIII, No. 3, July-September, 1983, p. 407.
8. *Ibid.*, p. 413.
9. F.S. Bagi, "Economics of Irrigation Crop Production in Haryana", *Indian Journal of Agricultural Economics*, Vol. XXXVI, No. 3, July-September, 1981.

10. K.C. Borach, "Factor Shares in Traditional Farming in Assam — A Case Study in Majuli – A River Island", *Indian Journal of Agricultural Economics*, Vol. XXXVIII, No. 3, July-September, 1983, p. 438.
11. P.S. Lalitha, "Technological Improvement — Labour Contribution and Its Share", *Indian Journal of Agricultural Economics*, Vol. XXXVIII, No. 3, July-September, 1983, p. 443.
12. L.J. Lau and P.A. Yotopoulos, "Profit Supply and Factor Demand Functions", *American Journal of Agricultural Economics*, Vol. 54, No. 1, February, 1972, pp. 11-18.
13. A.A. Walters, "Production and Cost Functions: An Econometric Survey", *Econometrica*, Vol. 31, Nos. 1-2, January-April, 1963, pp. 1-66.
14. P. Binswanger, "The Measurement of Technical Change Biases with Many Factors of Production", *The American Economic Review*, Vol. LXIV, No. 5, December 1974, pp. 964-976.

# CHAPTER 7

# Summary of Findings Conclusion and Suggestions

## INTRODUCTION

Pulses occupy a prominent place in Indian agriculture. The area under pulses in the country is the largest, accounting for about one-third of the world's area under the crop. Since Independence, the Indian Government has been emphasising the importance of agricultural development. The New Agricultural Strategy (NAS) was initiated in 1966. Accordingly, policies were formulated to utilize and promote high yielding crops of food grains in all districts selected under the IADF and IAAP schemes. The NAS was first introduced in the karif season of 1966. It also came to be known as the High Yielding Crops Programme (HYCP). The persistent efforts made by the Indian agricultural scientists since the introduction of HYCP resulted in the evolution of numerous high-yielding crops of principal crops and new farm practices.

Under HYCP, varietal improvement helps packing into the seed and ability to yield more for a given situation. The implementation of HYCP has brought about an increase in pulses production. Pulses are the most important food crop of Tamil Nadu. The introduction of High-Yielding Crops

Programmes in the mid-60s brought about a significant increase in production and productivity of food grains in the State. Hence, in the present study an attempt has been made to study the cost and returns of pulses namely black gram and green gram cultivation in Thoothukudi district.

Thoothukudi district in Tamil Nadu State is one of the most important districts where there has been a significant progress for cultivating pulses. Pulses are mainly cultivated in almost all the seven taluks in this district.

The main objective of the study is to analyse the cost and returns, determinants of yield and supply responsiveness of selected pulses production in Thoothukudi district. The specific objectives of the study are:

1. To analyse the cost and return structure of black and green grams and of small and large farmers producing black and green grams.
2. To identify and analyse the determinants of yield and factors causing yield gap with regard to farmers cultivating two crops of pulses and of small and large farmers group.
3. To estimate and analyse the input demand elasticities and supply responsiveness of two group of farmers cultivating black and green grams.
4. To investigate the labour absorption capacity and supply responsiveness of each crop with regard to their own prices and prices of variable inputs and units of fixed inputs.
5. To study the nature and returns to scale for both black and green grams cultivating farmers.

A random sample of 300 farmers, 150 each from BG and Green Gram cultivators of pulses was selected from 15 villages of three blocks in Thoothukudi District. These 300 sample farmers were selected randomly by adopting proportionate random sampling technique from 15 villages.

The sample farmers in each crop were classified into Large and Small farmer groups. Those cultivating an area of five acres and more were grouped under the Small farmer category, while those cultivating less than five acres of land were classified as large farmers. There were 98 Large farmers and 52 Small farmers in the case of Black Gram whereas in the case of Green Gram 103 and 47 were under Large and Small farmer groups respectively. The homogeneity with respect to net income per acre of these two crops namely Black Gram and Green Gram of pulses is examined by using the analysis of variance technique. It was found that there existed significant difference between them and they were treated as a separate unit for further analysis.

In the foregoing chapters, the characteristics of the selected farmers, cost and returns structure, determinants of yield, yield gap and yield constraints, input demand elasticities, supply responsiveness, and labour absorption, have been discussed. The major findings along with conclusions and suggestions are now presented in this chapter.

## SUMMARY OF FINDINGS

### Cost and Return Structure

A study of the input and output structure at mean levels of Large and Small farmers producing Black Gram of pulses revealed that Small farmers obtained significantly larger yield per acre than the Large farmers. The significant difference between two groups of farmers was found with respect to chemical fertilizers and pesticides. The yield reaped by Large farmers was relatively less compared to Small farmers in the study area. At the same time, the inputs namely fertilizers and pesticides used by Large farmers were found to be higher than their counterpart. Similar results were also observed in the case of Large and Small farmers cultivating Green Gram of pulses. But a comparison of the levels of input use and yield obtained per acre by two farmer groups in each crop revealed a higher yield and more uses of inputs in the case of Black Gram than the Green Gram. Thus, it is observed that the cultivation of Black Gram required a higher level of fertilizer application and lower level of pesticides due to its greater responsiveness to the output. Further, a Small farmer is likely to have a greater interest in maximizing his farm output than the Large farmer and pulses cultivation normally needs a quite close supervision which is easier on Small farms. A Small farmer is more likely to have an intimate knowledge of his farmland and its requirements. These help to increase the production efficiency on Small farmers in both crops in the study area.

Thus, it may be concluded from the analysis that the Small farmers were efficient in the use of inputs and they produced more yield than the Large farmers.

Pulses cultivation in general was found to be labour intensive in the study area. The analysis of utilisation of labour in both crops revealed the fact that the cultivation of Black Gram of pulses at Small farmer can help to provide gainful employment to the rural population under both farmer groups.

The analysis of cost and returns structure in the farmers cultivating Black Gram (BG) and Green Gram (GG) of pulses revealed that the Large farmers received higher returns amounting to Rs.4760.81 in the case of BG and Rs.6163.34 in the case of GG. The yield per acre of Large farmers was 181.61 kgs and it was 194.12 kgs in the case Small farmers producing BG of pulses. Whereas in the case GG of pulses, the yield per acre was 182.31 kgs for Large farmers and 196.12 kgs for Small farmers. Thus, it is inferred that the BG crop yielded higher returns in physical and monetary terms and it is found, to be more profitable than the Green Gram in the study area. It was also observed from the analysis that Large farmers spent higher amount per acre and received lesser net returns compared to Small farmers in both varieties.

The variable cost formed about 86 per cent of the total cost in both varieties. Human labour, the major cost component, accounted for nearly 39 per cent of the total cost. The pattern of other input expenditures was almost similar to the two varieties.

Thus, it may be concluded from the analysis that the yield per acre of Small farmers was significantly higher than that of the Large operator. This may be due to the more intensive use of inputs and better personal supervision and farm management by Small farmers for both varieties.

An examination of the economics of pulses cultivation showed that each rupee spent resulted in a benefit 1.82 in the case of Large farmers and 1.98 in the case Small farmers cultivating BG of pulses. Whereas in the case of GG of pulses, it was 2.13 and 2.48 for Large and Small farmers respectively. It indicated that this could be the outcome of better economies and institutional position of Small farmers compared with those of Large farmers in the study area.

**Determinants of Yield, Yield Gap and Yield Constraints**

A Cobb-Douglas type of multiple regression models was fitted to identify the major determinants of yield of Large and Small farmer groups cultivating BG and GG of pulses. The five independent crops chosen to explain the variations in the yield of pulses were:

1. human labour;
2. bullock labour;
3. fertilizer;
4. pesticides; and
5. capital flows.

In the case of Large and Small farmers cultivating Black Gram of pulses, all the five independent variables jointly explained about 79 to 81 per cent of the variations in the yield of pulses. Among the significant variables, human labour had a greater influence on the determination of yield in the case of Small farmers, it was followed by fertilizer. The fitted regression model emerged highly significant.

In the case of Small farmers, the impact of capital flows on yield of pulses was found to be higher and it was followed by the variable human labour. The fitted regression model was statistically significant at five per cent level. In overall case, capital flows were found to be the most influential input on yield determinations of Black Gram of pulses.

In order to examine whether structural difference existed between Large and Small farmers cultivating Black Gram, Chow's Test was applied. The results revealed that there existed structural difference between the two groups of farmers. Further, it is observed that there is a neutral technical change between the two farmer groups. At slope level, variable fertilizer was responsible for the difference in their yield. Thus, it may be concluded that the use of fertilizers differentiated in yield of Large and Small farmers cultivating Black Gram of pulses in the study area.

The regression analysis for Green Gram revealed that the independent variables caused about 78 to 81 per cent of the variations in the yield per acre. The variables, human labour, fertilizer and capital flows were significantly related to yield for both farmer groups. Fertilizer and capital flows were found to be the most influential variables in the determination of yield for Large and Small farmers respectively. The fitted regression model was statistically significant at five per cent level.

The examination of the structural differences between Large and Small farmers revealed that there existed a structural difference between Large and Small farmers in the study area. The analysis based on dummy variables revealed the existence of structural difference between two groups at slope level. At the slope level, input namely capital flows were responsible for the differences in yield. At the intercept level, the co-efficient of dummy variable was not statistically significant, indicating that there was a neutral technical change between the two farmer groups in the study area.

The analysis of yield gap revealed the existence of a gap between the potential and actual yield per acre for both farmer groups in each category of group. The yield gap was found higher in the case of Small farmers than in the case of Large farmers.

The Garrett's ranking technique was applied to identify the major constraints to the attainment of potential yield and it was found that severity of disease and pest attacks and water shortage were identified as major constraints for both Large and Small farmers cultivating BG of pulses . In the case Green Gram, Large farmers have reported that the inadequate credit facilities and water shortage to be the main constraints to maximum yield. Similarly, the majority of the Small farmers have identified water shortage as a major constraint. Thus, it may be concluded that severity of diseases, inadequate credit facilities and water shortage were identified as major constraints in the study area.

## Analysis of Input Demand Elasticities and Supply Responsiveness

The analysis of labour demand elasticities revealed that labour demand was highly sensitive to changes in pulses price for both Large and Small farmers in each category. The demand for labour with regard to real wage rate was elastic in both cases. It is observed from the analysis that increase in farm wage had a relatively serious negative effect on the demand for labour. In other words, 10 per cent reduction in the wage rate could increase labour employment by more than 10 per cent. But in practice, wage reduction may not be possible in order to increase farm employment. Comparing these two varieties, the reduction was found high in the case of GG than BG of pulses cultivation.

It is also observed from the analysis that the negative and low responsiveness of labour demand resulted in an increase in the price of bullock pairs, fertilizers and pesticides which indicated that manipulation of input price was not effective. Increase in area under pulses of both crops had favourable effects on labour demand while the impact of changes in capital flows was low.

The analysis of the demand for variable inputs in response to changes in their own prices for both groups in each crop revealed that demand for variable inputs was elastic and sensitive to changes in their own prices. The cross price elasticities of the inputs were negative and low for both farmer groups in each variety. It indicates that these variables were complements rather than substitutes.

Regarding the supply responsiveness, supply elasticities were highly sensitive to price changes in pulses for both farmer groups under each category. The negative and low responsiveness of output supply resulted in an increase in prices of variable inputs namely human labour, fertilizer and pesticides. Fixed factors produce a favourable impact on the same for both farmer groups. Capital flows had a higher impact on Small farmers than on Large farmers in BG and GG of pulses in the study area.

The indirect estimates for the groups of farmers in both crops revealed that land and human labour were the dominant factors. It is evident from the analysis that the share of land of total output was the highest for Large and Small farmers.

In both cases, the constant returns to scale were found to prevail with respect to production of BG and GG of pulses in the study area. Regarding technical change and factor shares, the results indicate that share of land is the maximum in pulses cultivation of both the varieties. It is found that there is a difference between the two crops regarding the share of land in output. The labour share of output is found to be higher for BG than GG. Therefore, the share of labour decreases substantially as one move from Green Gram to Black Gram. It indicates that it is due to efficiency gain in the cultivation of pulses in terms of labour under Black Gram compared to Green Gram. In the case of capital the Black Gram requires more of capital inputs than the Green Gram. The share of capital is found to be high in BG and GG.

## CONCLUSION

Thus, it is concluded from the analysis that small farmers are economically more efficient than large farmers irrespective of varieties of pulses cultivation in the study area. This could be due to the better supervision and more efficient farm management favoured by the smaller size of operational holdings. This indicated that apart from the efficient allocation of inputs, direct supervision and farm management are crucial determinants of economic efficiency.

## SUGGESTIONS

It is suggested on the basis of the findings that the extension service officials may improve technical efficiency by advising the farmers on input application at the proper time as recommended.

The farmers in the study area were of the opinion that they could not achieve the maximum yield due to the severity of diseases and pest attacks. It is suggested that the farmers should be educated properly to apply the pesticides at the prescribed level and this may be possible by the agricultural department officer attached to the panchayat unions.

Non-availability of credit was the other constraint. It is suggested that financial institutions should revitalise and revamp the existing credit facilities in the study area so that the farmers could get timely credit for undertaking improved cultivation practices.

Such measures shall certainly pave the way for the farmer's greater success.

The marketing cost constitutes a major portion of the consumer prices. Hence, Government should encourage the farmers to start co-operative societies in the study area in order to develop a direct link between the wholesalers/ retailers, processors and exporters to cut down the marketing cost incurred for lengthy channel.

Majority of the farmers prefer middlemen to sell their produce because of the credit facilities extended by them. The long chain of channels affects the procurement prices of pulses. Therefore, the Government should direct the co-operative and commercial banks in the study area to provide adequate loan facilities at a reasonable rate of interest to the farmers without any rigid formalities.

To sum up, a long term arrangement should be worked out by the Government of Tamil Nadu, to protect the interest of both producers and consumers of pulses and also to improve the production and marketing of pulses in the study area. It is also very essential to note that the prices offered to farmers are related to the cost of production. Further, a new mechanism has to be innovated to break the stagnation in the production of pulses through adoption of the most modern methods of cultivation and to ensure stable remunerative prices to the farmers. The Government should initiate action to improve market information system and market intelligence. Existing techniques disseminating marketing information should be reviewed. Visual media like television can be used for providing market information to farmers of rural areas. Modern devices such as computers may be employed wherever necessary to make a meaningful estimate of marketable surplus and daily average prices.

# Bibliography


## BOOKS

Acharya, S.S and Agarwal, N.L., *Agricultural Marketing in India*, Oxford and IBH Publishing Company, New Delhi, 1987.

Aiyaswamy P.K., et.al., *Pattern of Labour Utilization, Wage Structure and Labour Productivity in Selected Regions of Tamil Nadu*, Tamil Nadu Agricultural University, Coimbatore, 1974.

Bhalla, G.S., and Gurmal Singh, *Indian Agriculture*, Sage Publications, New Delhi, 2001.

Bhattacharjee, *Reflection on the Approach to Studies in Farm Economics in India*, Indian Society of Agricultural Economics, Bombay ,1961.

Bishop, C.E., and Joussunit, *Agricultural Twin Analysis*, John Willey and Sons, Inc., New York, 1958.

Curtis, R.C. *Economics for the Student*, Leonard Hill, London, 1963.

Fure M. and D.L. McFadden, *Production Economics*, A Dual Approach to Theory and Application Noth-Holland Publishing Company Amsterdam, 1978.

Handerson J.M. and R.E. Quandt, *Micro-Economic Theory – A Mathematical Approach*, McGraw Hill Kogakusha Limited, Tokyo, 1971.

Hanson, J.C. *A Text Book of Economics*, Leonard Hill, London,1972.

Jawahar Thakur D.K Singh and MiloRoy "An Analysis of Trends Growth and Technological Development Oilseed in Bihar.

Kanniyan, S.Proceedings and Recommendations on Increasing Productivity of Pulses in Tamil Nadu-Seminar Proceedings on 22-9-2000.

Zellner, A "A Efficient Method for Estimating Seemingly Unrelated Regression and Test for Aggregation Bias", Vol. 57, No. 2, June 1962.

## JOURNALS

Abhi, M.R. Kumar P. and V.C. Mathur, "Technological Change and Factor Shares in Cotton Production: A Case Study of Akola Cotton Farms", *Indian Journal of Agricultural Economics,* Vol. XXXVIII, No. 3, July-September, 1983.

Allan Gowar, "Productivity in Canadian Agriculture", *Canadian Journal of Agricultural Economics*, 28(2), 1980.

Ansari A. A. and s. A. Ismail, "Paddy Cultivation In Sodic Soil Through Vermitech", *International Journal of Sustainable Crop Production,* Vol. 3(5) August 2008.

Basavaraja, H. Mahajanashetti S.B. and P. Sivanagaraju, "Technological Change in Paddy Production: A Comparative Analysis of Traditional and SRI Methods of Cultivation", *Indian Journal of Agricultural Economics,* Research Notes, Vol. 63, No. 4, October-December 2008.

Bhattacharjee, J.P. "Resource-use and Productivity in World Agriculture", *Journal of Farm Economics*, 37(1), 1955.

Bishop C.E. and W.D. Joussunit, *Agricultural Twin Analysis,* John Wiley and Sons, Inc., New York, 1958.

Davidson B.R. and B.R. Martin, "The Relationship between Yields on Farms and in Experiments", *Australian Journal of Agricultural Economics*, Vol. 9, No. 2, December 1965.

Earl O. Heady, "Returns to Scale and Farm Size, Economics of Agricultural Productivity and Resource-use", *Journal of Farm Economics*, 34(2), 1952.

Fale, J.B. Jahakare G.G. and S.G. Borude, "An Economic Analysis of Yield Gap in Rice in Retnagiri District", *Agricultural Situation in India*, Vol. 39, No. 2, 1985.

Flinn J.C. and Mubarak Ali, "Technical Efficiency in Basmati Rice Production", *Pakistan Journal of Applied Economics*, Vol. 5, No. 1, 1986.

Junankar, P.N. "Do Indian Farmers Maximise Profit?", *The Journal of Development Studies*, Vol. 17, No. 1, October 1980.

Kahlon S.S. and H.S. Sandhu, "Economic Evaluation of Dry Farming in Punjab", *Indian Journal of Agricultural Economics*, 26(4), 1971.

Kalirajan K. and J.C. Flinn, "Allorative Efficiency and Supply Response in Irrigated Rice Production", *Indian Journal of Agricultural Economics*, Vol. 36, No. 2, April-June, 1981.

Kalirajan, K. "The Contribution of Location Specific Research to Agricultural Productivity", *Indian Journal of Agricultural Economics*, Vol. 35, No. 4, October-December, 1980.

Kalirajan, K. "The Economic Efficiency of Farmers Growing High Yielding, Irrigated Rice in India", *American Journal of Agricultural Economics*, August, 1981.

Kargoanker, M.C. "Productivity: A Systems Approach", *Productivity*, 18(1), 1977.

Kaul J.L. and S.K. Mehta, "Movement of Relative Shares of Factors of Production in Total Agricultural Income — A Study of Punjab Farmers", *Indian Journal of Economics*, 53(208), 1972.

Kohls R.L. and W.D. Damey, *Marketing of Agricultural Product*, Mac Millan Company, New York, 1972.

Kumar, L.R. Srinivas K. and S.R.K. Singh, "Technical Efficiency of Rice Farms under Irrigated Conditions of North West Himalayan Region — A Non-Parametric Approach", *Indian Journal of Agricultural Economics*, Vol. 60, No3, July-September, 2005.

Lau L.J. and P.A. Yolopoulos, "A Test for Relative Economic Efficiency and Application to Indian Agriculture", *American Economic Review*, Vol. 61, March, 1971.

Lau L.J. and P.A. Yolopoulos, "Profit Supply and Factor Demand Functions", *American Journal of Agricultural Economics*, Vol. 54, No. 1, February 1972.

Lavanya, S.J. Bala Rao M.M. and A.A. Pandu Ranga Rao, "Farm Finance by Banks – A Sample Study", *Eastern Economist*, 15(2), 1976.

Lawrence R. Klein, *An Introduction to Econometrics*, Prentice-Hall of India Private Limited, New Delhi, 1973.

Mahesh Chand, "On using Cobb-Douglas Production Function in Agriculture with Reference to India", *Indian Journal of Economics*, 48(189), 1967.

Mokheyi, K.K. Gap Analysis-An Effective Production Increase Concept in Rice, *Summary of a Lecture Delivered at the State Leaven Training Meeting on Rice*, held at Purila Department of Agriculture West Bengal, India July, 1977.

Pan A. Yolopoulos and L.J. Lau, "Resource use in Agriculture Application of the Profit Function to Selected Countries", *Food Research Institute Studies*, Vol. 17, No. 1, 1979.

Paul A. Samuelson, *Economics*, McGraw Hill, Kogakusha Limited, Tokyo, 1973.

Rajagopalan V. et.al., *Studies on Cost of Production in Tamil Nadu*, Department of Agricultural Economics, Tamil Nadu Agricultural University Coimbatore, 1978.

Rajagopalan V. et.al. Studies on Cost of Production of major crops in Tamil Nadu, *Department of Agricultural Economics*, Tamil Nadu Agriculture University, Coimbatore, 1978.

Ramesh Gupta, "Income Raising Potential on Rainfed Farm in Jabalpur District, Madhya Pradesh", *Indian Journal of Agricultural Economics*, 26(4), 1971.

Sampath, R.K. 'Nature and Measurement of Economic Efficiency in Indian Agriculture", *Indian Journal of Agricultural Economics*, Vol. 34, No. 2, April-June, 1979.

Sampath, R.K. *Economic Efficiency in Indian Agriculture*, The Macmillan Company, Delhi, 1979.

Shappand, F.W. *Cost and Production Function*, Princeton University Pren, Prinedon, 1953.

Sharma S.K Sharma H.R and Sharma R.K Trends in Area Production and Yield of Commercial Crops in Indian Agricultural with Special Reference to Oil Seeds Agricultural Situation in India 44 (7); .1989

Shivamurthy, M. Ramakrishna Rao, L. Shailaja Hittalamani and M. T. Lakshminarayan, "Constraints of Farmers Cultivating Rainfed Paddy in Eastern Dry Zone of Karnataka", *Mysore Journal of Agricultural Science*, Vol. 42(1), 2008.

Shukla, B.D. "Input-Output Relationship in Agriculture" *Indian Journal of Agricultural Economics*, Vol. 21, No. 3, 1966.

State Level Seminar on Increasing Productivity of Pulses in Tamil Nadu National Pulse Research Centre 22-9-2000 by Mr. K. Seerangan

Subramanian G and Vasanthi S.P "Agricultural Trends in Tamil Nadu 1961 to 1978 Agricultural Situation in India 43 (1);. 1988.

Subramanian K.V Growth of Horticulture Crops in India, Constrains and Opportunities Agriculture Situation in India39 (5),. 1984.

Subramaniyan G. and V. Nirmala, "Yield Gap Analysis in Rice Cultivation", *Southan Economist*, Vol. 27, No. 15, 1988.

Suresh A. and T.R. Keshava Reddy, "Resource-use efficiency of Paddy Cultivation in Peechi Command Area of Thrissur District of Kerala: An Economic Analysis", *Agricultural Economics Research Review*, Vol. 19, January-June, 2006.

Survey of Cost Production of Raw Cotton, *42nd Planary Meeting of the International Cotton Advisory Committee*, Memphis, USA Vol. 10, October 1983.

Suryawanshi S.D. and N.S. Gaikward, "An Analysis of Yield Gap in Rabi Jowar in Drought Prone Area of Ahmednagar District", *Agricultural Situation in India*, Vol. 39, No. 3, 1984.

Tandon R.K. and S.P. Dhondyal, *Principles and Methods of Farm Management*, Nirbal-Kebal-Ram Press, Kanpur, 1978.

Wanchai, K. Gomaz, A. "Basic Concepts, Objects and Approach Constraints to High Yields on Siren Rice Farms", *An Interim Report*, (Manila: International Rice Research Institute), 1977.

Yadav P.N. and A.C. Gangwar, "Rice Production and Constraints in Bihar State", *Agricultural Situation in India*, Vol. 12, No. 1, 1986.

Yolopoulos P.A. and L.J. Lau, "A Test for Relative Economic Efficiency: Some Further Results", *The American Economic Review*, Vol. LXIII, No. 1, March 1973.

## UNPUBLISHED PH.D., THESIS

Chandrasekaran, C.M. Yield Gap Analysis in Sugarcane Crop in Awanashi Taluk, Coimbatore District (Unpublished M.Sc., (Agri) Thesis Submitted to Department of Agricultural Economics, Tamil Nadu agricultural University, Coimbatore, 1985), pp. 96-97.

David Groenfeldt, "Appreciating the Hidden Values of Paddy Cultivation Towards a New Policy Framework for Agriculture", *INWEPF/SY*/2004(03).

David Rajarekan, D. *Yield Gap Analysis: A Study of Selected Crops in Madurai District* (*Paddy, Cholam, Cumbu, Groundnut*) (Unpublished M.Sc. (Agri) Thesis Submitted to Tamil Nadu Agricultural University, Coimbatore 1984), pp.148-149.

Lakshmanan, R. *Constraints in Irrigated Groundnut: An Analytical Study of Yield and Technological Gap*, (Unpublished Ph.D Thesis, Tamil Nadu Agricultural University, Coimbatore, 1986).

Minutes-Paper Submitted by Gouroru on Tropical Soils in TNAV@ National Pulse Research centre.

Tripathy, A. *A Study of Technological Gap in Adoption of New Rice Technology in Coolstal Orissa and Constraints Responsible for the Same*, (Unpublished Ph.D. Thesis, Indian Agricultural Research Institute, New Delhi, 1977).

## REPORTS

AGROSTAT, Joint Director of Agriculture, Thoothukudi, 2003.

Census of India, 1991, District Census Hand Book, Thoothukudi.

Season and Crop Reports of Tamil Nadu Department of Economics and Statistics, Chennai – Several Issues.

Statistical Hand Book, District Statistical Office, Thoothukudi.

Statistical Hand Book of Tamil Nadu, 1995.

Studies in Economics of Farm Management in Coimbatore District, Directorate of Economics and Statistics, Tamil Nadu, Report for the year 1971-1972.

## WEBSITES

www.emeraldinside.com

www.googlee.com

www.india.agronet.com

www.tn.gov.in.com

# Index


**A**

Analysis of
- black gram, 117
- cost and return structure, 73-95
- green gram, 124
- input demand elasticities and supply responsiveness, 146

Analytical framework, 96, 115

**B**

Black Gram, 96

**C**

Ceteris paribus, 129

Characteristics of sample farmers, 73
- age-wise distribution, 73-74
- distribution of family size, 75-76
- distribution of size of operational holdings, 78-79
- family members engaged in cultivation, 77
- farming experience of sample farmers, 79
- literacy levels, 74-75

Cobb-Douglas Production Function, 115

Comparative analysis of BG and GG farmers groups, 136
- demand for labour, 136
- factor shares, 137-138
- returns to scale, 137
- supply responsiveness, 136-137

Cost and return structure, 84, 142
- cost and returns structure of black gram, 85-88
- cost and returns structure of green gram, 89-95
- cost components, 84-85
- economics of cultivating black gram, 88-89

**D**

Determinants of yield, yield gap and constraints, 96-114

Dhranga Dhara Chemical, 66

**E**

Estimated results of regression model for black gram, 98, 102

Exotic Modern Variety (EMV), 41

**F**

FAO/WHO, 6

Findings, 140-157

**G**

Green Gram, 96

Green revolution, 3

**H**

Harvest, 13

Harvesting, 15

Heavy Water Plant, 66

High Yielding Crops Programme (HYCP), 140

Hybrid seed production in red gram for COPH 2, 14

**I**

Impact of black gram on factor shares, 131

- absolute factor shares in total income, 135-136
- measurement of production elasticities, 132-134
- nature of bias, 134-135
- nature of factors bias and factor shares in total income, 134

Impact of black gram on input demand elasticities, supply responsiveness, labour absorption and factor shares, 115-139

Indian Council for Agricultural Research, 4

Indian Government, 140

Indian Institute of Pulses Research Kanpur, 46

Indirect estimates of production elasticities, 122, 129

Indo-Gangetic plains, 3

International Cotton Advisory Committee, 28

Introduction, 1-23

Invigouration, 10

Irrigation, 12

Isolation distance, 15

**L**

Labour utilisation and input output structure, 80

- input-output structure, 82-84
- labour utilisation, 80-82

Land Development Bank, 85

Land requirement, 9

Limitations of the study, 22

**M**

Maintenance of purity, 12

Methodology and profile of the study area, 58-72

Methodology, 58

- administrative regions, 63
- climate and rainfall, 64-65
- collection of data, 59-60
- cropping pattern, 72
- district at a glance, 63
- fisheries, 66
- forestry, 66
- industries, 66
- irrigation, 69-72
- land-use pattern, 67
- method of analysis, 60
- operational holdings, 67-68
- period of the study, 60
- population characteristics, 63-64
- port, 66
- profile of the study area, 63
- rivers, 65
- sample design, 58-59
- soils and minerals, 65
- tools of analysis, 60-62
- transport and communication, 66

N

National Food Security Mission, 20
New Agricultural Strategy (NAS), 140
Normalized Profit Function, 115

O

Objectives of the study, 21
Own and cross price elasticities of demand for
labour, 125
variable inputs, 127
Own and cross price elasticities of output supply green gram, 128

P

Planting ratio, 14
Pre-harvest sanitation spray, 13
Pulses cultivation in Thoothukudi district, 19
Pulses production in India, 2
Pulses production in Tamil Nadu, 17

R

Recent trends in seed production in pulses, 9
Review of literature and concepts, 24-57
Ansari, 31
Bassvaraja, 31
Chandrasekaran, 36
concepts, 47
cost c includes the following items, 50
cost, 49
fixed costs, 50-51
Flinn, 37
Groenfeldt, David, 29
Kalirajan, 42
Kanniayan, S., 45
Kaul, 51
Kumar, 29
Kumar, 41
Lakshman, 38
Mehta, 51
production function, 48
production, 47
productivity, 48-49
Rajagopalan, 25
Rajasekar, David, 25
Reddy, T.R. Keshava, 30
research gap, 47
returns, 51
Seerangan, K., 45
Shivamurthy, M., 33
Shukla, 25
studies relating to
cost of production, 24-34
profit function approach, 39-45
pulses, 45-47
yield gap and yield constraints, 34-38
Subramanian, 46
Tandon, 51
test for absolute price efficiency of
large farms, 44-45
small farms, 44
test for equal relative
economic efficiency, 43
price efficiency, 43
technical and price efficiency, 43

Tripathy, 35
variable cost, 49-50
Yadav, 37
yield constraints, 38-39
Rhizonbium, 11
Rice fallow pulses, 7
Rogueing, 15

**S**

Seed hardening-cum-invigouration treatment of pulses, 9
Seed hardening-pre-conditioning, 10
Seed processing, 14
Seed storage and treatment techniques in pluses, 16
Seed treatment, 14
Seeds and sowing, 9
Soaking and drying, 10
Southern Petro-Chemical Industries Company, 66
Sowing, 15
Statement of the problem, 20
Suggestions, 148
Supply and demand elasticities, 118

**T**

Technical Efficiency of Rice Farms, 29
Test for structural differences, 100, 104
Tests of the stability of intercept and scope, 100, 105

**U**

Unit Output Price, 132
Uttar Pradesh, 3

**Y**

Yield constraints, 109
Yield gap and yield constraints, 106